PEOPLE'S POCKET LECTIONARY
For Sundays in Year 2 (1970)

This book contains the Sunday readings for 1970 from the new cycle of readings, the New Lectionary, promulgated by Pope Paul VI. It gives the Christian people, who take part in the celebration of Mass, Sunday by Sunday, the opportunity of hearing the most important parts of the revealed word of God.

Three readings are given for Sundays:
  i. a first reading from the Old Testament
  ii. a second reading from an apostle
  iii. a third reading from the Gospel.

In the Lectionary itself, these readings follow a three year cycle; in 1970, the readings provided for Year 2 are used.

At each season of the year (Advent, Christmastide, Lent, Easter, Pentecost), the readings follow the theme of the season.

During the Sundays of the Year which fall outside particular seasons, semi-continuous readings from a particular Gospel are given, so that the people may become familiar with the entire Gospel; the Old Testament readings are chosen for the light they throw on the Gospel readings; and the readings from the letters of the Apostles are also semi-continuous.

The chants between the readings: after each reading, a chant is given. To follow the reading from the Old Testament, a psalm is said or sung, the people making a response to each stanza. To precede the Gospel, there is either an Alleluia verse or, during Lent, an Acclamation.

The people are encouraged to join in the celebration of the Word by attentive listening to the readings and, where appropriate, by saying or singing the parts allotted to them, with understanding and devotion.

John E. Bartholomew
(℅ Choir, St Peter's, Falcon Avenue)

PEOPLE'S POCKET LECTIONARY

For Sundays in Year 2 (1970)

Containing all the new readings and
the chants between the readings

Jerusalem Bible Texts and Grail Psalms

 GEOFFREY CHAPMAN
LONDON DUBLIN MELBOURNE 1969

Geoffrey Chapman Ltd
18 High Street, Wimbledon, London SW19

Geoffrey Chapman (Ireland) Ltd
5–7 Main Street, Blackrock, County Dublin

Geoffrey Chapman Pty Ltd
346 St Kilda Rd, Melbourne, Vic 3004, Australia

Imprimatur: ✠ Patrick Casey V.G. Westminster
8.9.69.

English edition, made in Great Britain by
C. Nicholls & Company Ltd.
Irish edition, made in Ireland.

CONTENTS

Advent

Christmastide

Sundays of the Year

Lent

Paschaltide

Sundays of the Year (ctd)

1st Sunday of Advent

First Reading   Isaiah 63:16–17; 64:1.3–8
Oh, that you would tear the heavens open and come down.

You, Lord, yourself are our Father,
Our Redeemer is your ancient name.
Why, Lord, leave us to stray from your ways
and harden our hearts against fearing you?
Return, for the sake of your servants,
the tribes of your inheritance.
Oh, that you would tear the heavens open and come down
—at your Presence the mountains would melt.
No ear has heard,
no eye has seen
any god but you act like this
for those who trust him.
You guide those who act with integrity
and keep your ways in mind.
You were angry when we were sinners;
we had long been rebels against you.
We were all like men unclean,
all that integrity of ours like filthy clothing.
We have all withered like leaves
and our sins blew us away like the wind.
No one invoked your name
or roused himself to catch hold of you.
For you hid your face from us
and gave us up to the power of our sins.
And yet, Lord, you are our Father;
we the clay, you the potter,
we are all the work of your hand.
    This is the word of the Lord.

Responsorial Psalm
Ps 79:2–3.15–16.18–19.
R. v. 4

1. O shepherd of Israel, hear us,
shine forth from your cherubim throne.
O Lord, rouse up your might,
O Lord, come to our help.

Response
God of hosts, bring us back:
let your face shine on us and we shall be saved.

2. God of hosts, turn again, we implore,
look down from heaven and see.
Visit this vine and protect it,
the vine your right hand has planted. (*R.*)

3. May your hand be on the man you have chosen,
the man you have given your strength.
And we shall never forsake you again:
give us life that we may call upon your name. (*R.*)

Second Reading
1 Cor 1:3–9
We are waiting for our Lord Jesus Christ to be revealed.

May God our Father and the Lord Jesus Christ send you grace and peace.

I never stop thanking God for all the graces you have received through Jesus Christ. I thank him that you have been enriched in so many ways, especially in your teachers and preachers; the witness to Christ has indeed been strong among you so that you will not be without any of the gifts of the Spirit while you are waiting for our Lord Jesus Christ to be revealed; and he will keep you steady and without blame until the last day, the day of our Lord Jesus Christ, because God by calling you has joined you to his Son, Jesus Christ; and God is faithful.

This is the word of the Lord.

Alleluia Ps 84:8

Alleluia, alleluia!
Let us see, O Lord, your mercy
and give us your saving help.
Alleluia!

Gospel Mk 13:33–37
*Stay awake, because you do not know when the master
of the house is coming.*

Jesus said to his disciples: "Be on your guard, stay
awake, because you never know when the time will
come. It is like a man travelling abroad: he has gone
from home, and left his servants in charge, each with
his own task; and he has told the doorkeeper to stay
awake. So stay awake, because you do not know
when the master of the house is coming, evening,
midnight, cockcrow, dawn; if he comes unexpectedly,
he must not find you asleep. And what I say to you I
say to all: Stay awake!"
  This is the Gospel of the Lord.

2nd Sunday of Advent

First Reading Isaiah 40:1–5.9–11
Prepare a way for the Lord.

"Console my people, console them"
says your God.
"Speak to the heart of Jerusalem
and call to her
that her time of service is ended,

3

that her sin is atoned for,
that she has received from the hand of the Lord
double punishment for all her crimes."
A voice cries, "Prepare in the wilderness
a way for the Lord.
Make a straight highway for our God
across the desert.
Let every valley be filled in,
every mountain and hill be laid low,
let every cliff become a plain,
and the ridges a valley;
then the glory of the Lord shall be revealed
and all mankind shall see it;
for the mouth of the Lord has spoken."
Go up on a high mountain,
joyful messenger to Zion.
Shout with a loud voice,
joyful messenger to Jerusalem.
Shout without fear,
say to the towns of Judah,
"Here is your God."
Here is the Lord coming with power,
his arm subduing all things to him.
The prize of his victory is with him,
his trophies all go before him.
He is like a shepherd feeding his flock,
gathering lambs in his arms,
holding them against his breast
and leading to their rest the mother ewes.
    This is the word of the Lord.

Responsorial Psalm   Ps 84:9–14. *R.* v. 8

1. I will hear what the Lord God has to say,
a voice that speaks of peace,
peace for his people.

His help is near for those who fear him
and his glory will dwell in our land.

Response
Let us see, O Lord, your mercy,
and give us your saving help.

2. Mercy and faithfulness have met;
justice and peace have embraced.
Faithfulness shall spring from the earth
and justice look down from heaven. (*R.*)

3. The Lord will make us prosper
and our earth shall yield its fruit.
Justice shall march before him
and peace shall follow his steps. (*R.*)

Second Reading   2 Peter 3:8–14
We are waiting for the new heavens and new earth.

There is one thing, my friends, that you must never
forget: that with the Lord, "a day" can mean a thousand
years, and a thousand years is like a day. The Lord is
not being slow to carry out his promises, as anybody
else might be called slow; but he is being patient with
you all, wanting nobody to be lost and everybody to be
brought to change his ways. The Day of the Lord will
come like a thief, and then with a roar the sky will vanish,
the elements will catch fire and fall apart, the earth
and all that it contains will be burnt up.
   Since everything is coming to an end like this, you
should be living holy and saintly lives while you wait
and long for the Day of God to come, when the sky
will dissolve in flames and the elements melt in the
heat. What we are waiting for is what he promised:
the new heavens and new earth, the place where

5

righteousness will be at home. So then, my friends, while you are waiting, do your best to live lives without spot or stain so that he will find you at peace.

This is the word of the Lord.

Alleluia
Lk 3 :4.6

Alleluia, alleluia !
Prepare a way for the Lord,
make his paths straight.
And all mankind shall see the salvation of God.
Alleluia !

Gospel
Mk 1 :1–8

Make his paths straight.

The beginning of the Good News about Jesus Christ, the Son of God. It is written in the book of the prophet Isaiah:
Look, I am going to send my messenger before you;
he will prepare your way.
A voice cries in the wilderness:
Prepare a way for the Lord,
make his paths straight,
and so it was that John the Baptist appeared in the wilderness, proclaiming a baptism of repentance for the forgiveness of sins. All Judaea and all the people of Jerusalem made their way to him, and as they were baptised by him in the river Jordan they confessed their sins. John wore a garment of camel-skin, and he lived on locusts and wild honey. In the course of his preaching he said, "Someone is following me, someone who is more powerful than I am, and I am not fit to kneel down and undo the strap of his sandals. I have baptised you with water, but he will baptise you with the Holy Spirit."

This is the Gospel of the Lord.

3rd Sunday of Advent

First Reading   Isaiah 61 :1–2 .10–11
I exult for joy in the Lord.

The spirit of the Lord has been given to me,
for the Lord has anointed me.
He has sent me to bring good news to the poor,
to bind up hearts that are broken ;
to proclaim liberty to captives,
freedom to those in prison ;
to proclaim a year of favour from the Lord.
"I exult for joy in the Lord,
my soul rejoices in my God,
for he has clothed me in the garments of salvation,
he has wrapped me in the cloak of integrity,
like a bridegroom wearing his wreath,
like a bride adorned in her jewels.
For as the earth makes fresh things grow,
as a garden makes seeds spring up,
so will the Lord make both integrity and praise
spring up in the sight of the nations."
  This is the word of the Lord.

Responsorial Psalm   Lk 1 :46–50 . 53–54 . *R.*
                                         Is 61 :10

1. My soul glorifies the Lord,
my spirit rejoices in God, my Saviour.
He looks on his servant in her nothingness ;
henceforth all ages will call me blessed.

  Response
  My soul rejoices in my God.

7

2. The Almighty works marvels for me.
Holy his name !
His mercy is from age to age,
on those who fear him. (*R.*)

3. He fills the starving with good things,
sends the rich away empty.
He protects Israel, his servant,
remembering his mercy. (*R.*)

Second Reading   Thess. 5 :16–24
*May you all be kept safe, spirit, soul and body, for the
coming of the Lord.*

Be happy at all times; pray constantly; and for all
things give thanks to God, because this is what God
expects you to do in Christ Jesus.

Never try to suppress the Spirit or treat the gift of
prophecy with contempt; think before you do anything
—hold on to what is good and avoid every form of evil.

May the God of peace make you perfect and holy;
and may you all be kept safe and blameless, spirit, soul
and body, for the coming of our Lord Jesus Christ. God
has called you and he will not fail you.

This is the word of the Lord.

Alleluia   Lk 4 :18

Alleluia, alleluia !
The spirit of the Lord has been given to me.
He has sent me to bring good news to the poor.
Alleluia !

Gospel   Jn 1:6–8.19–28

*There stands among you—unknown to you—the one who
is coming after me.*

A man came, sent by God.
His name was John.
He came as a witness,
as a witness to speak for the light,
so that everyone might believe through him.
He was not the light,
only a witness to speak for the light.

This is how John appeared as a witness. When the
Jews sent priests and Levites from Jerusalem to ask
him, "Who are you?" he not only declared, but he
declared quite openly, "I am not the Christ." "Well then,"
they asked "are you Elijah?" "I am not" he said. "Are you
the Prophet?" He answered, "No." So they said to him,
"Who are you? We must take back an answer to those
who sent us. What have you to say about yourself?"
So John said, "I am, as Isaiah prophesied:

a voice that cries in the wilderness:
Make a straight way for the Lord."

Now these men had been sent by the Pharisees, and
they put this further question to him, "Why are you
baptising if you are not the Christ, and not Elijah, and
not the prophet?" John replied, "I baptise with water;
but there stands among you—unknown to you—the
one who is coming after me; and I am not fit to undo
his sandal-strap." This happened at Bethany, on the far
side of the Jordan, where John was baptising.

This is the Gospel of the Lord.

4th Sunday of Advent

First Reading   2 Sam 7:1–5.8–11.16
The kingdom of David will always stand secure before the Lord.

Once David had settled into his house and the Lord had given him rest from all the enemies surrounding him, the king said to the prophet Nathan, "Look, I am living in a house of cedar while the ark of God dwells in a tent." Nathan said to the king, "Go and do all that is in your mind, for the Lord is with you."

But that very night the word of the Lord came to Nathan:

"Go and tell my servant David, 'Thus the Lord speaks: Are you the man to build me a house to dwell in? I took you from the pasture, from following the sheep, to be leader of my people Israel; I have been with you on all your expeditions; I have cut off all your enemies before you. I will give you fame as great as the fame of the greatest on earth. I will provide a place for my people Israel; I will plant them there and they shall dwell in that place and never be disturbed again; nor shall the wicked continue to oppress them as they did, in the days when I appointed judges over my people Israel; I will give them rest from all their enemies. The Lord will make you great; the Lord will make you a House. Your House and your sovereignty will always stand secure before me and your throne be established for ever.'"

This is the word of the Lord.

Responsorial Psalm   Ps 88 :2–5 . 27 . 29. *R.* v. 2

1. I will sing for ever of your love, O Lord ;
through all ages my mouth will proclaim your truth.
Of this I am sure, that your love lasts for ever,
that your truth is firmly established as the heavens.

   Response
   I will sing for ever of your love, O Lord.

2. "I have made a covenant with my chosen one ;
I have sworn to David my servant :
I will establish your dynasty for ever
and set up your throne through all ages." (*R.*)

3. He will say to me : "You are my father,
my God, the rock who saves me."
I will keep my love for him always ;
for him my covenant shall endure. (*R.*)

Second Reading   Rom 16 :25–27
*The mystery, which was kept secret for endless ages, is
now made clear.*

Glory to him who is able to give you the strength to
live according to the Good News I preach, and in which
I proclaim Jesus Christ, the revelation of a mystery kept
secret for endless ages, but now so clear that it must
be broadcast to pagans everywhere to bring them to the
obedience of faith. This is only what scripture has
predicted, and it is all part of the way the eternal God
wants things to be. He alone is wisdom ; give glory
therefore to him through Jesus Christ for ever and
ever. Amen.
   This is the word of the Lord.

Alleluia Lk 1:38

Alleluia, alleluia!
I am the handmaid of the Lord:
let what you have said be done to me.
Alleluia!

Gospel Lk 1:26–38
Listen! You are to conceive and bear a son.

In the sixth month the angel Gabriel was sent by God to a town in Galilee called Nazareth, to a virgin betrothed to a man named Joseph, of the House of David; and the virgin's name was Mary. He went in and said to her, "Rejoice, so highly favoured! The Lord is with you." She was deeply disturbed by these words and asked herself what this greeting could mean, but the angel said to her, "Mary, do not be afraid; you have won God's favour. Listen! You are to conceive and bear a son, and you must name him Jesus. He will be great and will be called Son of the Most High. The Lord God will give him the throne of his ancestor David; he will rule over the House of Jacob for ever and his reign will have no end." Mary said to the angel, "But how can this come about, since I am a virgin?" "The Holy Spirit will come upon you" the angel answered "and the power of the Most High will cover you with its shadow. And so the child will be holy and will be called Son of God. Know this too: your kinswoman Elizabeth has, in her old age, herself conceived a son, and she whom people called barren is now in her sixth month, for nothing is impossible to God." "I am the handmaid of the Lord," said Mary "let what you have said be done to me." And the angel left her.
    This is the Gospel of the Lord.

The Nativity of Our Lord

25 December

Midnight Mass

First Reading   Isaiah 9:1–7
A Son is given to us.

The people that walked in darkness
has seen a great light;
on those who live in a land of deep shadow
a light has shone.
You have made their gladness greater,
you have made their joy increase;
they rejoice in your presence
as men rejoice at harvest time,
as men are happy when they are dividing the spoils.
For the yoke that was weighing on him,
the bar across his shoulders,
the rod of his oppressor,
these you break as on the day of Midian.
For all the footgear of battle,
every cloak rolled in blood,
is burnt
and consumed by fire.
For there is a child born for us,
a son given to us
and dominion is laid on his shoulders;
and this is the name they give him:
Wonder-Counsellor, Mighty-God,
Eternal-Father, Prince-of-Peace.
Wide is his dominion

in a peace that has no end,
for the throne of David
and for his royal power,
which he establishes and makes secure
in justice and integrity.
From this time onwards and for ever,
the jealous love of the Lord of hosts will do this.
    This is the word of the Lord.

Responsorial Psalm   Ps 95:1–3.11–13. *R.* Lk 2:11

1. O sing a new song to the Lord,
sing to the Lord all the earth.
O sing to the Lord, bless his name.

Response
Today a saviour has been born to us:
he is Christ the Lord.

2. Proclaim his help day by day,
tell among the nations his glory
and his wonders among all the peoples. (*R.*)

3. Let the heavens rejoice and earth be glad,
let the sea and all within it thunder praise,
let the land and all it bears rejoice,
all the trees of the wood shout for joy
at the presence of the Lord for he comes,
he comes to rule the earth. (*R.*)

4. With justice he will rule the world,
he will judge the peoples with his truth. (*R.*)

Second Reading   Titus 2:11–14
God's grace has been revealed to the whole human race.

God's grace has been revealed, and it has made salvation possible for the whole human race and taught us
that what we have to do is to give up everything that
does not lead to God, and all our worldly ambitions;
we must be self-restrained and live good and religious
lives here in this present world, while we are waiting in
hope for the blessing which will come with the Appearing
of the glory of our great God and saviour Christ Jesus.
He sacrificed himself for us in order to set us free from
all wickedness and to purify a people so that it could be
his very own and would have no ambition except to do
good.
    This is the word of the Lord.

Alleluia   Lk 2:10–11

Alleluia, alleluia!
I bring you news of great joy:
today a saviour has been born to us, Christ the Lord.
Alleluia!

Gospel   Lk 2:1–14
Today a saviour has been born to you.

Now at this time Caesar Augustus issued a decree for a
census of the whole world to be taken. This census—
the first—took place while Quirinius was governor of
Syria, and everyone went to his own town to be
registered. So Joseph set out from the town of Nazareth
in Galilee and travelled up to Judaea, to the town of
David called Bethlehem, since he was of David's House
and line, in order to be registered together with Mary, his

betrothed, who was with child. While they were there the time came for her to have her child, and she gave birth to a son, her first-born. She wrapped him in swaddling clothes, and laid him in a manger because there was no room for them at the inn. In the countryside close by there were shepherds who lived in the fields and took it in turns to watch their flocks during the night. The angel of the Lord appeared to them and the glory of the Lord shone round them. They were terrified, but the angel said, "Do not be afraid. Listen, I bring you news of great joy, a joy to be shared by the whole people. Today in the town of David a saviour has been born to you ; he is Christ the Lord. And here is a sign for you : you will find a baby wrapped in swaddling clothes and lying in a manger." And suddenly with the angel there was a great throng of the heavenly host, praising God and singing :
"Glory to God in the highest heaven,
and peace to men who enjoy his favour."

This is the Gospel of the Lord.

25 December.   Dawn Mass

First Reading   Isaiah 62 :11–12
Look, your saviour comes.

This the Lord proclaims
to the ends of the earth :
Say to the daughter of Zion, "Look,
your saviour comes,
the prize of his victory with him,
his trophies before him".
They shall be called "The Holy People",
"The Lord's Redeemed".
And you shall be called "The-sought-after",
"City-not-forsaken".

This is the word of the Lord.

Responsorial Psalm   Ps 96:1.6.11–12

1. The Lord is king, let earth rejoice,
the many coastlands be glad.
The skies proclaim his justice;
all peoples see his glory.

> *Response*
> This day new light will shine upon the earth:
> the Lord is born for us.

2. Light shines forth for the just
and joy for the upright of heart.
Rejoice, you just, in the Lord;
give glory to his holy name. (*R.*)

Second Reading   Titus 3:4–7
It was for no reason except his own compassion that he saved us.

When the kindness and love of God our saviour for
mankind were revealed, it was not because he was
concerned with any righteous actions we might have
done ourselves; it was for no reason except his own
compassion that he saved us, by means of the cleans-
ing water of rebirth and by renewing us with the Holy
Spirit which he has so generously poured over us
through Jesus Christ our saviour. He did this so that
we should be justified by his grace, to become heirs
looking forward to inheriting eternal life.
    This is the word of the Lord.

Alleluia

Lk 2:14

Alleluia, alleluia!
Glory to God in the highest heaven,
and peace to men who enjoy his favour.
Allelulia!

Gospel

2:15–20

The shepherds found Mary and Joseph and the baby.

Now when the angels had gone from them into heaven, the shepherds said to one another, "Let us go to Bethlehem and see this thing that has happened which the Lord has made known to us." So they hurried away and found Mary and Joseph, and the baby lying in the manger. When they saw the child they repeated what they had been told about him, and everyone who heard it was astonished at what the shepherds had to say. As for Mary, she treasured all these things and pondered them in her heart. And the shepherds went back glorifying and praising God for all they had heard and seen; it was exactly as they had been told.

This is the Gospel of the Lord.

Christmas Day Mass

First Reading

Isaiah 52:7–10

All the ends of the earth shall see the salvation of our God.

How beautiful on the mountains,
are the feet of one who brings good news,
who heralds peace, brings happiness,
proclaims salvation,

and tells Zion,
"Your God is king !"
Listen ! Your watchmen raise their voices,
they shout for joy together,
for they see the Lord face to face,
as he returns to Zion.
Break into shouts of joy together,
you ruins of Jerusalem ;
for the Lord is consoling his people,
redeeming Jerusalem.
The Lord bares his holy arm
in the sight of all the nations,
and all the ends of the earth shall see
the salvation of our God.
 This is the word of the Lord.

Responsorial Psalm   Ps 97 :1–6. *R*. v. 3

1. Sing a new song to the Lord
for he has worked wonders.
His right hand and his holy arm
have brought salvation.

 Response
 All the ends of the earth have seen
 the salvation of our God.

2. The Lord has made known his salvation ;
has shown his justice to the nations.
He has remembered his truth and love
for the house of Israel. (*R*.)

3. All the ends of the earth have seen
the salvation of our God.
Shout to the Lord all the earth,
ring out your joy. (*R*.)

4. Sing psalms to the Lord with the harp,
with the sound of music.
With trumpets and the sound of the horn
acclaim the King, the Lord. (*R.*)

Second Reading   Heb 1 :1–6
God has spoken to us through his Son.

At various times in the past and in various different
ways, God spoke to our ancestors through the prophets ;
but in our own time, the last days, he has spoken to us
through his Son, the Son that he has appointed to
inherit everything and through whom he made everything
there is. He is the radiant light of God's glory and the
perfect copy of his nature, sustaining the universe by his
powerful command ; and now that he has destroyed
the defilement of sin, he has gone to take his place in
heaven at the right hand of divine Majesty. So he is now
as far above the angels as the title which he has inherited
is higher than their own name.

God has never said to any angel : You are my Son,
today I have become your father, or : I will be a father
to him and he a son to me. Again, when he brings the
First-born into the world, he says : Let all the angels of
God worship him.

This is the word of the Lord.

Alleluia

Alleluia, alleluia !
A hallowed day has dawned upon us.
Come, you nations, worship the Lord,
for today a great light has shone down upon the earth.
Alleluia !

Gospel Jn 1 :1—18

The Word was made flesh, and lived among us.

In the beginning was the Word :
the Word was with God
and the Word was God.
He was with God in the beginning.
Through him all things came to be,
not one thing had its being but through him.
All that came to be had life in him
and that life was the light of men,
a light that shines in the dark,
a light that darkness could not overpower.
A man came, sent by God.
His name was John.
He came as a witness,
as a witness to speak for the light,
so that everyone might believe through him.
He was not the light,
only a witness to speak for the light.
The Word was the true light
that enlightens all men ;
and he was coming into the world.
He was in the world
that had its being through him,
and the world did not know him.
He came to his own domain
and his own people did not accept him.
But to all who did accept him
he gave power to become children of God,
to all who believe in the name of him
who was born not out of human stock
or urge of the flesh
or will of man
but of God himself.
The Word was made flesh,

he lived among us,
and we saw his glory,
the glory that is his as the only Son of the Father,
full of grace and truth.
John appears as his witness. He proclaims:
"This is the one of whom I said:
He who comes after me
ranks before me
because he existed before me."
Indeed, from his fulness we have, all of us, received—
yes, grace in return for grace,
since, though the Law was given through Moses,
grace and truth have come through Jesus Christ.
No one has ever seen God;
it is the only Son, who is nearest to the Father's heart,
who has made him known.

This is the Gospel of the Lord.

Sunday in the Octave of Christmas

Feast of the Holy Family

First Reading   Eccles 3:2–6.12–14
He who fears the Lord respects his parents.

The Lord honours the father in his children,
and upholds the rights of a mother over her sons.
Whoever respects his father is atoning for his sins,
he who honours his mother is like someone amassing
    a fortune.
Whoever respects his father will be happy with children
    of his own.
he shall be heard on the day when he prays.
Long life comes to him who honours his father,

he who sets his mother at ease is showing obedience to
the Lord.
My son, support your father in his old age,
do not grieve him during his life.
Even if his mind should fail, show him sympathy,
do not despise him in your health and strength;
for kindness to a father shall not be forgotten
but will serve as reparation for your sins.
This is the word of the Lord.

Responsorial Psalm   Ps. 127:1–5. *R.* v. 1

1. O blessed are those who fear the Lord
and walk in his ways!
By the labour of your hands you shall eat.
You will be happy and prosper.

Response
O blessed are those who fear the Lord
and walk in his ways!

2. Your wife like a fruitful vine
in the heart of your house;
your children like shoots of the olive,
around your table. (*R.*)

3. Indeed thus shall be blessed
the man who fears the Lord
May the Lord bless you from Zion
all the days of your life! (*R.*)

Second Reading   Col 3:12–21
Family life in the Lord.

You are God's chosen race, his saints; he loves you
and you should be clothed in sincere compassion, in

kindness and humility, gentleness and patience. Bear with one another; forgive each other as soon as a quarrel begins. The Lord has forgiven you; now you must do the same. Over all these clothes, to keep them together and complete them, put on love. And may the peace of Christ reign in your hearts, because it is for this that you were called together as parts of one body. Always be thankful.

Let the message of Christ, in all its richness, find a home with you. Teach each other, and advise each other, in all wisdom. With gratitude in your hearts sing psalms and hymns and inspired songs to God; and never say or do anything except in the name of the Lord Jesus, giving thanks to God the Father through him.

Wives, give way to your husbands, as you should in the Lord. Husbands, love your wives and treat them with gentleness. Children, be obedient to your parents always, because that is what will please the Lord. Parents, never drive your children to resentment or you will make them feel frustrated.

This is the word of the Lord.

Alleluia   Col 3:15.16

Alleluia, alleluia !
May the peace of Christ reign in your hearts ;
let the message of Christ find a home with you.
Alleluia !

Gospel   Lk 2:22–40
The child grew, filled with wisdom.

And when the day came for them to be purified as laid down by the Law of Moses, they took him up to

Jerusalem to present him to the Lord—observing what stands written in the Law of the Lord: Every first-born male must be consecrated to the Lord—and also to offer in sacrifice, in accordance with what is said in the Law of the Lord, a pair of turtledoves or two young pigeons. Now in Jerusalem there was a man named Simeon. He was an upright and devout man; he looked forward to Israel's comforting and the Holy Spirit rested on him. It had been revealed to him by the Holy Spirit that he would not see death until he had set eyes on the Christ of the Lord. Prompted by the Spirit he came to the Temple; and when the parents brought in the child Jesus to do for him what the Law required, he took him into his arms and blessed God; and he said:

"Now, Master, you can let your servant go in peace,
just as you promised;
because my eyes have seen the salvation
which you have prepared for all the nations to see,
a light to enlighten the pagans
and the glory of your people Israel."

As the child's father and mother stood there wondering at the things that were being said about him, Simeon blessed them and said to Mary his mother, "You see this child: he is destined for the fall and for the rising of many in Israel, destined to be a sign that is rejected—and a sword will pierce your own soul too—so that the secret thoughts of many may be laid bare."

There was a prophetess also, Anna the daughter of Phanuel, of the tribe of Asher. She was well on in years. Her days of girlhood over, she had been married for seven years before becoming a widow. She was now eighty-four years old and never left the Temple, serving God night and day with fasting and prayer. She came by just at that moment and began to praise

God; and she spoke of the child to all who looked forward to the deliverance of Jerusalem.

When they had done everything the Law of the Lord required, they went back to Galilee, to their own town of Nazareth. Meanwhile the child grew to maturity, and he was filled with wisdom; and God's favour was with him.

This is the Gospel of the Lord.

Octave of Christmas
and Solemnity of Mary Mother of God

1 January

First Reading   Num 6:22–27
They are to call down my name on the sons of Israel, and I will bless them.

The Lord spoke to Moses and said, "Say this to Aaron and his sons: 'This is how you are to bless the sons of Israel. You shall say to them:
May the Lord bless you and keep you.
May the Lord let his face shine on you and be gracious to you.
May the Lord uncover his face to you and bring you peace.'
This is how they are to call down my name on the sons of Israel, and I will bless them."

This is the word of the Lord.

Responsorial Psalm   Ps 66:2–3.5.6.8. *R*. v. 2

1. God, be gracious and bless us
and let your face shed its light upon us.

So will your ways be known upon earth
and all nations learn your saving help.

Response
O God, be gracious and bless us.

2. Let the nations be glad and exult
for you rule the world with justice.
With fairness you rule the peoples,
you guide the nations on earth. (*R.*)

3. Let the peoples praise you, O God;
let all the peoples praise you.
May God still give us his blessing
till the ends of the earth revere him. (*R.*)

Second Reading   Gal 4:4–7
God sent his Son, born of a woman.

When the appointed time came, God sent his Son,
born of a woman, born a subject of the Law, to redeem
the subjects of the Law and to enable us to be adopted as
sons. The proof that you are sons is that God has sent
the Spirit of his Son into our hearts; the Spirit that cries,
"Abba, Father", and it is this that makes you a son, you
are not a slave any more; and if God has made you son,
then he has made you heir.
    This is the word of the Lord.

Alleluia   Heb 1:1–2

Alleluia, Alleluia!
At various times in the past
and in various different ways,
God spoke to our ancestors through the prophets;

but in our own time, the last days,
he has spoken to us through his Son.
Alleluia !

Gospel   Lk 2 :16–21
They found Mary and Joseph and the baby . . . When the
eighth day came, they gave him the name Jesus.

The shepherds hurried away to Bethlehem and found
Mary and Joseph, and the baby lying in the manger.
When they saw the child they repeated what they had
been told about him, and everyone who heard it was
astonished at what the shepherds had to say. As for
Mary, she treasured all these things and pondered
them in her heart. And the shepherds went back
glorifying and praising God for all they had heard and
seen ; it was exactly as they had been told.

When the eighth day came and the child was to be
circumcised, they gave him the name Jesus, the name
the angel had given him before his conception.

This is the Gospel of the Lord.

2nd Sunday after Christmas

First Reading   Eccles 24 : 1–2. 8–12
The wisdom of God has pitched her tent among the
chosen people.

Wisdom speaks her own praises,
in the midst of her people she glories in herself.
She opens her mouth in the assembly of the Most High,
she glories in herself in the presence of the Mighty One.
Then the creator of all things instructed me,

and he who created me fixed a place for my tent.
He said, 'Pitch your tent in Jacob,
make Israel your inheritance.'
From eternity, in the beginning, he created me,
and for eternity I shall remain.
I ministered before him in the holy tabernacle,
and thus was I established on Zion.
In the beloved city he has given me rest,
and in Jerusalem I wield my authority.
I have taken root in a privileged people,
in the Lord's property, in his inheritance.
    This is the word of the Lord.

Responsorial Psalm Ps 147:12–15.19–20. *R*. Jn 1:14

1. O praise the Lord, Jerusalem!
Zion, praise your God!
He has strengthened the bars of your gates,
he has blessed the children within you.

   Response
   The Word was made flesh,
   and lived among us.

   Alternative Response
   Alleluia!

2. He established peace on your borders,
he feeds you with finest wheat.
He sends out his word to the earth
and swiftly runs his command. (*R*.)

3. He makes his word known to Jacob,
to Israel his laws and decrees.
He has not dealt thus with other nations;
he has not taught them his decrees.
Alleluia! (*R*.)

Second Reading Eph 1 :3–6 .15–18

He determined that we should become his adopted sons through Jesus.

Blessed be God the Father of our Lord Jesus Christ, who has blessed us with all the spiritual blessings of heaven in Christ. Before the world was made, he chose us, chose us in Christ, to be holy and spotless, and to live through love in his presence, determining that we should become his adopted sons, through Jesus Christ, for his own kind purposes, to make us praise the glory of his grace, his free gift to us in the Beloved.

That will explain why I, having once heard about your faith in the Lord Jesus, and the love that you show towards all the saints, have never failed to remember you in my prayers and to thank God for you. May the God of our Lord Jesus Christ, the Father of glory, give you a spirit of wisdom and perception of what is revealed, to bring you to full knowledge of him. May he enlighten the eyes of your mind so that you can see what hope his call holds for you, what rich glories he has promised the saints will inherit.

This is the word of the Lord.

Alleluia 1 Tim 3 :16

Alleluia, alleluia !
Glory to you, O Christ, proclaimed to the pagans ;
Glory be to you, O Christ, believed in by the world.
Alleluia !

Gospel Jn 1 :1–18

The Word was made flesh, and lived among us.

In the beginning was the Word :
the Word was with God
30

and the Word was God.
He was with God in the beginning.
Through him all things came to be,
not one thing had its being but through him.
All that came to be had life in him
and that life was the light of men,
a light that shines in the dark,
a light that darkness could not overpower.
A man came, sent by God.
His name was John.
He came as a witness,
as a witness to speak for the light,
so that everyone might believe through him.
He was not the light,
only a witness to speak for the light.
The Word was the true light
that enlightens all men;
and he was coming into the world.
He was in the world
that had its being through him,
and the world did not know him.
He came to his own domain
and his own people did not accept him.
But to all who did accept him
he gave power to become children of God,
to all who believe in the name of him
who was borne not out of human stock
or urge of the flesh
or will of man
but of God himself.
The Word was made flesh,
he lived among us,
and we saw his glory,
the glory that is his as the only Son of the Father,
full of grace and truth.
John appears as his witness. He proclaims:
"This is the one of whom I said:

He who comes after me
ranks before me
because he existed before me."
Indeed, from his fulness we have, all of us, received—
yes, grace in return for grace,
since, though the Law was given through Moses,
grace and truth have come through Jesus Christ.
No one has ever seen God;
it is the only Son. who is nearest to the Father's heart,
who has made him known.
    This is the Gospel of the Lord.

Epiphany

6 January

First Reading   Isaiah 60:1–6
Above you the glory of the Lord appears.

Arise, shine out, for your light has come,
the glory of the Lord is rising on you,
though night still covers the earth
and darkness the peoples.
Above you the Lord now rises
and above you his glory appears.
The nations come to your light
and kings to your dawning brightness.
Lift up your eyes and look round:
all are assembling and coming towards you,
your sons from far away
and your daughters being tenderly carried.
At this sight you will grow radiant,
your heart throbbing and full;
since the riches of the sea will flow to you,

the wealth of the nations come to you;
camels in throngs will cover you,
and dromedaries of Midian and Ephah;
everyone in Sheba will come,
bringing gold and incense
and singing the praise of the Lord.
  This is the word of the Lord.

Responsorial Psalm   Ps 71 :1–2 . 7–8 . 10–13. *R.* v. 11

1. O God, give your judgement to the king,
to a king's son your justice,
that he may judge your people in justice
and your poor in right judgement.

  Response
  All nations shall fall prostrate before you, O Lord.

2. In his days justice shall flourish
and peace till the moon fails.
He shall rule from sea to sea,
from the Great River to earth's bounds. (*R.*)

3. The kings of Tarshish and the sea coasts
shall pay him tribute.
The kings of Sheba and Seba
shall bring him gifts.
Before him all kings shall fall prostrate,
all nations shall serve him. (*R.*)

4. For he shall save the poor when they cry
and the needy who are helpless.
He will have pity on the weak
and save the lives of the poor. (*R.*)

Second Reading Eph 3:2–3.5–6
It has now been revealed that pagans share the same inheritance.

You have probably heard how I have been entrusted by God with the grace he meant for you, and that it was by a revelation that I was given the knowledge of the mystery. This mystery that has now been revealed through the Spirit to his holy apostles and prophets was unknown to any men in past generations; it means that pagans now share the same inheritance that they are parts of the same body, and that the same promise has been made to them, in Christ Jesus, through the gospel.
    This is the word of the Lord.

Alleluia Mt 2:2

Alleluia, alleluia!
We saw his star as it rose
and have come to do the Lord homage.
Alleluia!

Gospel Mt 2:1–12
We saw his star and have come to do the king homage.

After Jesus had been born in Bethlehem in Judaea during the reign of King Herod, some wise men came to Jerusalem from the east. "Where is the infant king of the Jews?" they asked. "We saw his star as it rose and have come to do him homage." When King Herod heard this he was perturbed, and so was the whole of Jerusalem. He called together all the chief priests and the scribes of the people, and enquired of them where

the Christ was to be born. "At Bethlehem in Judaea,"
they told him "for this is what the prophet wrote:
And you, Bethlehem, in the land of Judah
you are by no means least among the leaders of Judah,
for out of you will come a leader
who will shepherd my people Israel."
Then Herod summoned the wise men to see him privately.
He asked them the exact date on which the star had
appeared, and sent them on to Bethlehem. "Go and
find out all about the child," he said "and when you
have found him, let me know, so that I too may go
and do him homage." Having listened to what the king
had to say, they set out. And there in front of them was
the star they had seen rising; it went forward and
halted over the place where the child was. The sight of
the star filled them with delight, and going into the
house they saw the child with his mother Mary, and
falling to their knees they did him homage. Then,
opening their treasures, they offered him gifts of gold
and frankincense and myrrh. But they were warned in
a dream not to go back to Herod, and returned to their
own country by a different way.

This is the Gospel of the Lord.

Sunday after Epiphany
Feast of the Baptism of Our Lord

(1st Sunday of the Year)

First Reading   Isaiah 42:1–4.6–7
Here is my servant in whom my soul delights.

Thus says the Lord:
Here is my servant whom I uphold,

my chosen one in whom my soul delights.
I have endowed him with my spirit
that he may bring true justice to the nations.
He does not cry out or shout aloud,
or make his voice heard in the streets.
He does not break the crushed reed,
nor quench the wavering flame.
Faithfully he brings true justice;
he will neither waver, nor be crushed
until true justice is established on earth,
for the islands are awaiting his law.
I, the Lord, have called you to serve the cause of right;
I have taken you by the hand and formed you;
I have appointed you as covenant of the people and
   light of the nations.
to open the eyes of the blind,
to free captives from prison,
and those who live in darkness from the dungeon.
   This is the word of the Lord.

Responsorial Psalm   Ps 28 :1—4 . 9—10. *R*. v. 11

1. O give the Lord you sons of God,
give the Lord glory and power;
give the Lord the glory of his name.
Adore the Lord in his holy court.

Response
The Lord will bless his people with peace.

2. The Lord's voice resounding on the waters,
the Lord on the immensity of waters;
the voice of the Lord, full of power,
the voice of the Lord, full of splendour. (*R*.)

3. The God of glory thunders.
In his temple they all cry: "Glory!"
The Lord sat enthroned over the flood;
the Lord sits as king for ever. (R.)

Second Reading   Acts 10:34—38
God anointed him with the Holy Spirit.

Peter addressed Cornelius and his household: "The
truth I have now come to realise" he said "is that God
does not have favourites, but that anybody of any
nationality who fears God and does what is right is
acceptable to him.

"It is true, God sent his word to the people of Israel,
and it was to them that the good news of peace was
brought by Jesus Christ—but Jesus Christ is Lord of
all men. You must have heard about the recent
happenings in Judaea; about Jesus of Nazareth and
how he began in Galilee, after John had been preaching baptism. God had anointed him with the Holy
Spirit and with power, and because God was with him,
Jesus went about doing good and curing all who had
fallen into the power of the devil."

This is the word of the Lord.

Alleluia   Mk 9:8

Alleluia, alleluia!
The heavens opened and the Father's voice resounded
"This is my Son, the Beloved. Listen to him."
Alleluia!

Gospel   Mk 1 :7–11
You are my Son, the Beloved; my favour rests on you.

In the course of his preaching John the Baptist said,
"Someone is following me, someone who is more
powerful than I am, and I am not fit to kneel down and
undo the strap of his sandals. I have baptised you with
water, but he will baptise you with the Holy Spirit."

It was at this time that Jesus came from Nazareth in
Galilee and was baptised in the Jordan by John. No
sooner had he come up out of the water than he saw
the heavens torn apart and the Spirit, like a dove,
descending on him. And a voice came from heaven,
"You are my Son, the Beloved; my favour rests on you."

This is the Gospel of the Lord.

2nd Sunday of the Year*

First Reading   1 Sam 3:3–10.19
Speak, Lord, your servant is listening.

Samuel was lying in the sanctuary of the Lord where
the ark of God was, when the Lord called, "Samuel!
Samuel!" He answered, "Here I am". Then he ran to
Eli and said, "Here I am, since you called me." Eli said,
"I did not call. Go back and lie down." So he went
and lay down. Once again the Lord called, "Samuel!
Samuel!" Samuel got up and went to Eli and said,
"Here I am, since you called me." He replied, "I did
not call you, my son; go back and lie down." Samuel
had as yet no knowledge of the Lord and the word

---

*Falls on 18 January 1970.

of the Lord had not yet been revealed to him. Once again the Lord called, the third time. He got up and went to Eli and said, "Here I am, since you called me." Eli then understood that it was the Lord who was calling the boy, and he said to Samuel, "Go and lie down, and if someone calls say, 'Speak, Lord, your servant is listening.'" So Samuel went and lay down in his place.

The Lord then came and stood by, calling as he had done before, "Samuel! Samuel!" Samuel answered, "Speak, Lord, your servant is listening."

Samuel grew up and the Lord was with him and let no word of his fall to the ground.

This is the word of the Lord.

Responsorial Psalm   Ps 39:2.4.7–10. *R.* vv. 8.9

1. I waited, I waited for the Lord
and he stooped down to me;
he heard my cry.
He put a new song into my mouth,
praise of our God.

   Response
   Here I am Lord!
   I come to do your will.

2. You do not ask for sacrifice and offerings,
but an open ear.
You do not ask for holocaust and victim.
Instead, here am I. (*R.*)

3. In the scroll of the book it stands written
that I should do your will.
My God, I delight in your law
in the depth of my heart. (*R.*)

4. Your justice I have proclaimed
in the great assembly.
My lips I have not sealed;
you know it, O Lord. (*R.*)

Second Reading   1 Cor 6:13–15.17–20
Your bodies are members making up the body of Christ.

The body is not meant for fornication; it is for the
Lord, and the Lord for the body. God who raised the
Lord from the dead, will by his power raise us up too.

You know, surely, that your bodies are members
making up the body of Christ; anyone who is joined
to the Lord is one spirit with him.

Keep away from fornication. All the other sins are
committed outside the body; but to fornicate is to sin
against your own body. Your body, you know, is the
temple of the Holy Spirit, who is in you since you
received him from God. You are not your own property;
you have been bought and paid for. That is why you
should use your body for the glory of God.

This is the word of the Lord.

Alleluia   See pp. 184–6

Gospel   Jn 1:35–42
They saw where he lived, and stayed with him.

As John stood with two of his disciples, Jesus passed,
and John stared hard at him and said, "Look, there
is the lamb of God." Hearing this, the two disciples
followed Jesus. Jesus turned round, saw them following and said, "What do you want?" They answered,
"Rabbi,"—which means Teacher—"where do you live?"
"Come and see" he replied; so they went and saw

where he lived, and stayed with him the rest of that day. It was about the tenth hour.

One of these two who became followers of Jesus after hearing what John had said was Andrew, the brother of Simon Peter. Early next morning, Andrew met his brother and said to him, "We have found the Messiah"—which means the Christ—and he took Simon to Jesus. Jesus looked hard at him and said, "You are Simon son of John; you are to be called Cephas"—meaning Rock.

This is the Gospel of the Lord.

3rd Sunday of the Year

First Reading   Jonah 3:1–5.10
The people of Nineveh renounce their evil behaviour.

The word of the Lord was addressed a second time to Jonah: "Up!" he said "Go to Nineveh, the great city, and preach to them as I told you to." Jonah set out and went to Nineveh in obedience to the word of the Lord. Now Nineveh was a city great beyond compare: it took three days to cross it. Jonah went on into the city, making a day's journey. He preached in these words, "Only forty days more and Nineveh is going to be destroyed." And the people of Nineveh believed in God; they proclaimed a fast and put on sackcloth, from the greatest to the least.

God saw their efforts to renounce their evil behaviour. And God relented: he did not inflict on them the disaster which he had threatened.

This is the word of the Lord.

Responsorial Psalm   Ps 24:4–9. *R.* v. 4

1. Lord, make me know your ways.
Lord, teach me your paths.
Make me walk in your truth, and teach me:
for you are God my saviour.

   Response
   Lord, make me know your ways.

2. Remember your mercy, Lord,
and the love you have shown from of old.
In your love remember me,
because of your goodness, O Lord. (*R.*)

3. The Lord is good and upright.
He shows the path to those who stray,
He guides the humble in the right path;
he teaches his way to the poor. (*R.*)

Second Reading   1 Cor 7:29–31
The world as we know it is passing away.

Brothers, this is what I mean: our time is growing
short. Those who have wives should live as though
they had none, and those who mourn should live as
though they had nothing to mourn for; those who are
enjoying life should live as though there were nothing
to laugh about; those whose life is buying things
should live as though they had nothing of their own;
and those who have to deal with the world should not
become engrossed in it. I say this because the world
as we know it is passing away.
   This is the word of the Lord.

Alleluia   Mk 1 :15

Alleluia, alleluia !
The kingdom of God is close at hand ;
believe the Good News.
Alleluia !

Gospel   Mk 1 :14–20
Repent, and believe the Good News.

After John had been arrested, Jesus went into Galilee.
There he proclaimed the Good News from God. "The
time has come" he said "and the kingdom of God is
close at hand. Repent, and believe the Good News."
   As he was walking along by the Sea of Galilee he
saw Simon and his brother Andrew casting a net in
the lake—for they were fishermen. And Jesus said to
them, "Follow me and I will make you into fishers of
men." And at once they left their nets and followed him.
   Going on a little further, he saw James son of
Zebedee and his brother John ; they too were in their
boat, mending their nets. He called them at once and,
leaving their father Zebedee in the boat with the men
he employed, they went after him.
   This is the Gospel of the Lord.

4th Sunday of the Year

First Reading   Deut 18 :15–20
*I will raise up a prophet and I will put my words into his
mouth.*

Moses said to the people : "Your God will raise up for
you a prophet like myself, from among yourselves,

43

from your own brothers; to him you must listen. This is what you yourselves asked of the Lord your God at Horeb on the day of the Assembly. 'Do not let me hear again' you said 'the voice of the Lord my God, nor look any longer on this great fire, or I shall die'; and the Lord said to me, 'All they have spoken is well said. I will raise up a prophet like yourself for them from their own brothers; I will put my words into his mouth and he shall tell them all I command him. The man who does not listen to my words that he speaks in my name, shall be held answerable to me for it. But the prophet who presumes to say in my name a thing I have not commanded him to say, or who speaks in the name of other gods, that prophet shall die."

This is the word of the Lord.

Responsorial Psalm   Ps 94:1–2.6–9. *R*. v. 8

1. Come, ring out our joy to the Lord;
hail the rock who saves us.
Let us come before him, giving thanks,
with songs let us hail the Lord.

Response
O that today you would listen to his voice!
Harden not your hearts.

2. Come in; let us kneel and bend low;
let us kneel before the God who made us
for he is our God and we
the people who belong to his pasture,
the flock that is led by his hand. (*R*.)

3. O that today you would listen to his voice!
"Harden not your hearts as at Meribah,
as on that day at Massah in the desert

when your fathers put me to the test;
when they tried me, though they saw my work." (R.)

Second Reading
1 Cor 7:32–35

An unmarried woman can devote herself to the Lord's affairs; all she need worry about is being holy.

I would like to see you free from all worry. An unmarried man can devote himself to the Lord's affairs, all he need worry about is pleasing the Lord; but a married man has to bother about the world's affairs and devote himself to pleasing his wife: he is torn two ways. In the same way an unmarried woman, like a young girl, can devote herself to the Lord's affairs; all she need worry about is being holy in body and spirit. The married woman, on the other hand, has to worry about the world's affairs and devote herself to pleasing her husband. I say this only to help you, not to put a halter round your necks, but simply to make sure that everything is as it should be, and that you give your undivided attention to the Lord.

This is the word of the Lord.

Alleluia
See pp. 184–6

Gospel
Mk 1:21–28

He taught them with authority.

They went as far as Capernaum, and as soon as the sabbath came Jesus went to the synagogue and began to teach. And his teaching made a deep impression on them because, unlike the scribes, he taught them with authority.

In their synagogue just then there was a man

possessed by an unclean spirit, and it shouted, "What do you want with us, Jesus of Nazareth? Have you come to destroy us? I know who you are: the Holy One of God." But Jesus said sharply, "Be quiet! Come out of him!" And the unclean spirit threw the man into convulsions and with a loud cry went out of him. The people were so astonished that they started asking each other what it all meant. "Here is a teaching that is new" they said "and with authority behind it: he gives orders even to unclean spirits and they obey him." And his reputation rapidly spread everywhere, through all the surrounding Galilean countryside.

This is the Gospel of the Lord.

5th Sunday of the Year

First Reading   Job 7:1–4.6–7
Restlessly I fret till twilight falls.

Job began to speak:
Is not man's life on earth nothing more than pressed service,
his time no better than hired drudgery?
Like the slave, sighing for the shade,
or the workman with no thought but his wages,
months of delusion I have assigned to me,
nothing for my own but nights of grief.
Lying in bed I wonder, "When will it be day?"
Risen I think, "How slowly evening comes!"
Restlessly I fret till twilight falls.
Swifter than a weaver's shuttle my days have passed,
and vanished, leaving no hope behind.
Remember that my life is but a breath,
and that my eyes will never again see joy.
This is the word of the Lord.

Responsorial Psalm   Ps 146:1–6. *R.* v. 3

1. Alleluia!
Praise the Lord for he is good;
sing to our God for he is loving:
to him our praise is due.

  Response
  Praise the Lord who heals the broken-hearted.

  Alternative Response
  Alleluia!

2. The Lord builds up Jerusalem
and brings back Israel's exiles,
he heals the broken-hearted,
he binds up all their wounds.
He fixes the number of the stars;
he calls each one by its name. (*R.*)

3. Our Lord is great and almighty;
his wisdom can never be measured.
The Lord raises the lowly;
he humbles the wicked to the dust. (*R.*)

Second Reading   1 Cor 9:16–19.22–23
I should be punished if I did not preach the Gospel.

I do not boast of preaching the gospel, since it is a
duty which has been laid on me; I should be punished
if I did not preach it! If I had chosen this work myself,
I might have been paid for it, but as I have not, it is a
responsibility which has been put into my hands. Do
you know what my reward is? It is this: in my
preaching, to be able to offer the Good News free, and
not insist on the rights which the gospel gives me.

47

So though I am not a slave of any man I have made myself the slave of everyone so as to win as many as I could. For the weak I made myself weak. I made myself all things to all men in order to save some at any cost; and I still do this, for the sake of the gospel, to have a share in its blessings.

This is the word of the Lord.

Alleluia. See pp. 184–6

Gospel Mk 1 :29–39
He cured many who were suffering from diseases of one kind or another.

On leaving the synagogue, Jesus went with James and John straight to the house of Simon and Andrew. Now Simon's mother-in-law had gone to bed with fever, and they told him about her straightaway. He went to her, took her by the hand and helped her up. And the fever left her and she began to wait on them.

That evening, after sunset, they brought to him all who were sick and those who were possessed by devils. The whole town came crowding round the door, and he cured many who were suffering from diseases of one kind or another; he also cast out many devils, but he would not allow them to speak, because they knew who he was.

In the morning, long before dawn, he got up and left the house, and went off to a lonely place and prayed there. Simon and his companions set out in search of him, and when they found him they said, "Everybody is looking for you." He answered, "Let us go elsewhere, to the neighbouring country towns, so that I can preach there too, because that is why I came." And he went all through Galilee, preaching in their synagogues and casting out devils.

This is the Gospel of the Lord.

1st Sunday of Lent

First Reading   Gen 9 :8–15
God's covenant with Noah after he had saved him from
the waters of the flood.

God spoke to Noah and his sons, "See, I establish my
Covenant with you, and with your descendants after
you ; also with every living creature to be found with
you, birds, cattle and every wild beast with you:
everything that came out of the ark, everything that
lives on the earth. I establish my Covenant with you:
no thing of flesh shall be swept away again by the
waters of the flood. There shall be no flood to destroy
the earth again."

God said, "Here is the sign of the Covenant I make
between myself and you and every living creature with
you for all generations : I set my bow in the clouds
and it shall be a sign of the Covenant between me and
the earth. When I gather clouds over the earth and
the bow appears in the clouds, I will recall the
Covenant between myself and you and every living
creature of every kind. And so the waters shall never
again become a flood to destroy all things of flesh."

This is the word of the Lord.

Responsorial Psalm   Ps 24 :4–9. R. v. 10

1. Lord, make me know your ways.
Lord, teach me your paths.
Make me walk in your truth, and teach me :
for you are God my saviour.

49

Response
Your ways, Lord, are faithfulness and love
for those who keep your covenant.

2. Remember your mercy, Lord,
and the love you have shown from of old.
In your love remember me,
because of your goodness, O Lord. (*R.*)

3. The Lord is good and upright.
He shows the path to those who stray,
he guides the humble in the right path;
he teaches his way to the poor. (*R.*)

Second Reading

1 Peter 3 :18—22

That water is a type of the baptism which saves you now.

Christ himself, innocent though he was, died once for sins, died for the guilty, to lead us to God. In the body he was put to death, in the spirit he was raised to life, and, in the spirit, he went to preach to the spirits in prison. Now it was long ago, when Noah was still building that ark which saved only a small group of eight people "by water", and when God was still waiting patiently, that these spirits refused to believe. That water is a type of the baptism which saves you now, and which is not the washing off of physical dirt but a pledge made to God from a good conscience, through the resurrection of Jesus Christ, who has entered heaven and is at God's right hand, now that he has made the angels and Dominations and Powers his subjects.

This is the word of the Lord.

Acclamation

Mt 4 :4

Man does not live on bread alone,
but on every word that comes from the mouth of God.

Gospel   Mk 1 :12–15
Jesus was tempted by Satan, and the angels looked after him.

The Spirit drove Jesus out into the wilderness and he remained there for forty days, and was tempted by Satan. He was with the wild beasts, and the angels looked after him.

After John had been arrested, Jesus went into Galilee. There he proclaimed the Good News from God. "The time has come" he said "and the kingdom of God is close at hand. Repent, and believe the Good News."

This is the Gospel of the Lord.

2nd Sunday of Lent

First Reading   Gen 22 :1–2 . 9–13 . 15–18
The sacrifice of Abraham, our father in faith.

God put Abraham to the test. "Abraham, Abraham" he called. "Here I am" he replied. "Take your son," God said "your only child Isaac, whom you love, and go to the land of Moriah. There you shall offer him as a burnt offering, on a mountain I will point out to you."

When they arrived at the place God had pointed out to him, Abraham stretched out his hand and seized the knife to kill his son.

But the angel of the Lord called to him from heaven. "Abraham, Abraham" he said. "I am here" he replied. "Do not raise your hand against the boy" the angel said. "Do not harm him, for now I know you fear God. You have not refused me your son, your only son."

51

Then looking up, Abraham saw a ram caught by its horns in a bush. Abraham took the ram and offered it as a burnt-offering in place of his son.

The angel of the Lord called Abraham a second time from heaven. "I swear by my own self—it is the Lord who speaks—because you have done this, because you have not refused me your son, your only son, I will shower blessings on you, I will make your descendants as many as the stars of heaven and the grains of sand on the seashore. Your descendants shall gain possession of the gates of their enemies. All the nations of the earth shall bless themselves by your descendants, as a reward for your obedience."

This is the word of the Lord.

Responsorial Psalm   Ps 115:10.15–19. *R.* Ps 114:9

1. I trusted, even when I said:
"I am sorely afflicted."
O precious in the eyes of the Lord
is the death of his faithful.

    Response
    I will walk in the presence of the Lord
    in the land of the living.

2. Your servant, Lord, your servant am I;
you have loosened my bonds.
A thanksgiving sacrifice I make:
I will call on the Lord's name. (*R.*)

3. My vows to the Lord I will fulfil
before all his people,
in the courts of the house of the Lord,
in your midst, O Jerusalem. (*R.*)

Second Reading   Rom 8:31—34
God did not spare his own Son.

With God on our side who can be against us? Since
God did not spare his own Son, but gave him up to
benefit us all, we may be certain, after such a gift,
that he will not refuse anything he can give. Could
anyone accuse those that God has chosen? When
God acquits, could anyone condemn? Could Christ
Jesus? No! He not only died for us—he rose from
the dead, and there at God's right hand he stands and
pleads for us.
   This is the word of the Lord.

Acclamation   Mt 17:5

From the bright cloud the Father's voice was heard:
"This is my Son, the Beloved. Listen to him."

Gospel   Mk 9:2—10
This is my Son, the Beloved.

Six days later, Jesus took with him Peter and James
and John and led them up a high mountain where
they could be alone by themselves. There in their
presence he was transfigured: his clothes became
dazzlingly white, whiter than any earthly bleacher
could make them. Elijah appeared to them with Moses;
and they were talking with Jesus. Then Peter spoke
to Jesus. "Rabbi", he said "it is wonderful for us to be
here; so let us make three tents, one for you, one for
Moses and one for Elijah." He did not know what to
say; they were so frightened. And a cloud came,
covering them in shadow; and there came a voice

from the cloud, "This is my Son, the Beloved. Listen to him." Then suddenly, when they looked round, they saw no one with them any more but only Jesus.

As they came down the mountain he warned them to tell no one what they had seen, until after the Son of Man had risen from the dead. They observed the warning faithfully, though among themselves they discussed what "rising from the dead" could mean.

This is the Gospel of the Lord.

3rd Sunday of Lent *

First Reading   Ex 20:1–17
The Law was given through Moses.

God spoke all these words. He said, "I am the Lord your God who brought you out of the land of Egypt, out of the house of slavery.

"You shall have no gods except me.

"You shall not make yourself a carved image or any likeness of anything in heaven or on earth beneath or in the waters under the earth; you shall not bow down to them or serve them. For I, the Lord your God, am a jealous God and I punish the father's fault in the sons, the grandsons, and the great-grandsons of those who hate me; but I show kindness to thousands of those who love me and keep my commandments.

"You shall not utter the name of the Lord your God to misuse it, for the Lord will not leave unpunished the man who utters his name to misuse it.

"Remember the sabbath day and keep it holy. For six days you shall labour and do all your work, but the seventh day is a sabbath for the Lord your God. You shall do no work that day, neither you nor your son

* The readings for Year 1 may be used as alternatives.

nor your daughter nor your servants, men or women, nor your animals nor the stranger who lives with you. For in six days the Lord made the heavens and the earth and the sea and all that these hold, but on the seventh day he rested; that is why the Lord has blessed the sabbath day and made it sacred.

"Honour your father and your mother so that you may have a long life in the land that the Lord your God has given to you.

"You shall not kill.

"You shall not commit adultery.

"You shall not steal.

"You shall not bear false witness against your neighbour.

"You shall not covet your neighbour's house. You shall not covet your neighbour's wife, or his servant, man or woman, or his ox, or his donkey, or anything that is his."

This is the word of the Lord.

Responsorial Psalm   Ps 18:8–11. *R.* Jn 6:68

1. The law of the Lord is perfect,
it revives the soul.
The rule of the Lord is to be trusted,
it gives wisdom to the simple.

Response
You, Lord, have the message of eternal life.

2. The precepts of the Lord are right,
they gladden the heart.
The command of the Lord is clear,
it gives light to the eyes. (*R.*)

3. The fear of the Lord is holy,
abiding for ever.
The decrees of the Lord are truth
and all of them just. (*R.*)

4. They are more to be desired than gold,
than the purest of gold
and sweeter are they than honey,
than honey from the comb. (*R.*)

Second Reading   1 Cor 1 :22–25
*Here we are preaching a crucified Christ, an obstacle to
men, but to those who are called, the wisdom of God.*

And so, while the Jews demand miracles and the
Greeks look for wisdom, here are we preaching a
crucified Christ; to the Jews an obstacle that they
cannot get over, to the pagans madness, but to those
who have been called, whether they are Jews or Greeks,
a Christ who is the power and the wisdom of God.
For God's foolishness is wiser than human wisdom,
and God's weakness is stronger than human strength.
    This is the word of the Lord.

Acclamation *   Ezek 18 : 31
Shake off all your sins – it is the Lord who speaks – and
make yourselves a new heart and a new spirit.

Gospel   Jn 2 :13–25
Destroy this sanctuary, and in three days I will raise it up.

Just before the Jewish Passover Jesus went up to
Jerusalem, and in the Temple he found people selling
cattle and sheep and pigeons, and the money changers
sitting at their counters there. Making a whip out of
some cord, he drove them all out of the Temple, cattle

---

* Alternative Acclamations may be taken from the Weekdays of Lent.

and sheep as well, scattered the money changers' coins, knocked their tables over and said to the pigeon-sellers, "Take all this out of here and stop turning my Father's house into a market." Then his disciples remembered the words of scripture: Zeal for your house will devour me. The Jews intervened and said, "What sign can you show us to justify what you have done?" Jesus answered, "Destroy this sanctuary, and in three days I will raise it up." The Jews replied, "It has taken forty-six years to build this sanctuary: are you going to raise it up in three days?" But he was speaking of the sanctuary that was his body, and when Jesus rose from the dead, his disciples remembered that he had said this, and they believed the scripture and the words he had said.

During his stay in Jerusalem for the Passover many believed in his name when they saw the signs that he gave, but Jesus knew them all and did not trust himself to them; he never needed evidence about any man; he could tell what a man had in him.

This is the Gospel of the Lord.

4th Sunday of Lent *

First Reading   Chron 36:14–16.19–23
The wrath and mercy of God are revealed in the exile and in the release of his people.

All the heads of the priesthood, and the people too, added infidelity to infidelity, copying all the shameful practices of the nations and defiling the Temple that the Lord had consecrated for himself in Jerusalem. The Lord, the God of their ancestors, tirelessly sent them messenger after messenger, since he wished to

---

* The readings from Year 1 may be used as alternatives.

spare his people and his house. But they ridiculed the messengers of God, they despised his words, they laughed at his prophets, until at last the wrath of the Lord rose so high against his people that there was no further remedy.

Their enemies burned down the Temple of God, demolished the walls of Jerusalem, set fire to all its palaces, and destroyed everything of value in it. The survivors were deported by Nebuchadnezzar to Babylon; they were to serve him and his sons until the kingdom of Persia came to power. This is how the word of the Lord was fulfilled that he spoke through Jeremiah, "Until this land has enjoyed its sabbath rest, until seventy years have gone by, it will keep sabbath throughout the days of its desolation."

And in the first year of Cyrus king of Persia, to fulfil the word of the Lord that was spoken through Jeremiah, the Lord roused the spirit of Cyrus king of Persia to issue a proclamation and to have it publicly displayed throughout his kingdom: "Thus speaks Cyrus king of Persia, 'The Lord, the God of heaven, has given me all the kingdoms of the earth; he has ordered me to build him a Temple in Jerusalem, in Judah. Whoever there is among you of all his people, may his God be with him! Let him go up.' "

This is the word of the Lord.

Responsorial Psalm   Ps 136. *R*. v. 6

1. By the rivers of Babylon
there we sat and wept,
remembering Zion;
on the poplars that grew there
we hung up our harps.

Response
O let my tongue
cleave to my mouth
if I remember you not!

2. For it was there that they asked us,
our captors, for songs,
our oppressors, for joy.
"Sing to us," they said,
"one of Zion's songs." (*R.*)

3. O how could we sing
the song of the Lord
on alien soil?
If I forget you, Jerusalem,
let my right hand wither! (*R.*)

4. O let my tongue
cleave to my mouth
if I remember you not,
if I prize not Jerusalem
above all my joys! (*R.*)

Second Reading   Eph 2:4–10
You who were dead through your sins have been saved
through grace.

God loved us with so much love that he was generous
with his mercy: when we were dead through our sins,
he brought us to life with Christ—it is through grace
that you have been saved—and raised us up with him
and gave us a place with him in heaven, in Christ Jesus.
   This was to show for all ages to come, through his
goodness towards us in Christ Jesus, how infinitely
rich he is in grace. Because it is by grace that you have
been saved, through faith; not by anything of your

own, but by a gift from God; not by anything that
you have done, so that nobody can claim the credit.
We are God's work of art, created in Christ Jesus to
live the good life as from the beginning he had meant
us to live it.

This is the word of the Lord.

Acclamation Jn 3:16

God loved the world so much that he gave his only Son;
everyone who believes in him has eternal life.

Gospel Jn 3:14–21
*God sent his Son so that through him the world might be
saved.*

Jesus said to Nicodemus:
The Son of Man must be lifted up
as Moses lifted up the serpent in the desert,
so that everyone who believes may have eternal life in
   him.
Yes, God loved the world so much
that he gave his only Son,
so that everyone who believes in him may not be lost
but may have eternal life.
For God sent his Son into the world
not to condemn the world,
but so that through him the world might be saved.
No one who believes in him will be condemned;
but whoever refuses to believe is condemned already,
because he has refused to believe
in the name of God's only Son.
On these grounds is sentence pronounced:
that though the light has come into the world
men have shown they prefer
60

darkness to the light
because their deed were evil.
And indeed, everybody who does wrong
hates the light and avoids it,
for fear his actions should be exposed;
but the man who lives by the truth
comes out into the light,
so that it may be plainly seen that what he does is
   done in God."
   This is the Gospel of the Lord.

5th Sunday of Lent

First Reading Jer 31:31—34
I will make a new covenant and never call their sin to mind.

See, the days are coming—it is the Lord who speaks—
when I will make a new covenant with the House of
Israel (and the House of Judah), but not a covenant
like the one I made with their ancestors on the day I
took them by the hand to bring them out of the land
of Egypt. They broke that covenant of mine, so I had
to show them who was master. It is the Lord who
speaks. No, this is the covenant I will make with the
House of Israel when those days arrive—it is the Lord
who speaks. Deep within them I will plant my Law,
writing it on their hearts. Then I will be their God and
they shall be my people. There will be no further need
for neighbour to try to teach neighbour, or brother to
say to brother, "Learn to know the Lord!" No, they will
all know me, the least no less than the greatest—it is the
Lord who speaks—since I will forgive their iniquity
and never call their sin to mind.
   This is the word of the Lord.

Responsorial Psalm Ps 50:3–4.12–15. *R.* v. 12

1. Have mercy on me, God, in your kindness.
In your compassion blot out my offence.
O wash me more and more from my guilt
and cleanse me from my sin.

Response
A pure heart create for me, O God.

2. A pure heart create for me, O God,
put a steadfast spirit within me.
Do not cast me away from your presence,
nor deprive me of your holy spirit. (*R.*)

3. Give me again the joy of your help;
with a spirit of fervour sustain me,
that I may teach transgressors your ways
and sinners may return to you. (*R.*)

Second Reading Heb 5:7–9
*He learnt to obey and became the source of eternal
salvation.*

During his life on earth, Christ offered up prayer and
entreaty, aloud and in silent tears, to the one who had
the power to save him out of death, and he submitted
so humbly that his prayer was heard. Although he was
Son, he learnt to obey through suffering; but having
been made perfect, he became for all who obey him
the source of eternal salvation.

This is the word of the Lord.

Acclamation

Jn 12:26

If a man serves me, says the Lord, he must follow me,
wherever I am, my servant will be there too.

Gospel

Jn 12:20–33

*If a grain of wheat falls on the ground and dies, it yields
a rich harvest.*

Among those who went up to worship at the festival
were some Greeks. These approached Philip, who came
from Bethsaida in Galilee, and put this request to him,
"Sir, we should like to see Jesus." Philip went to tell
Andrew, and Andrew and Philip together went to
tell Jesus.

Jesus replied to them:
"Now the hour has come
for the Son of Man to be glorified.
I tell you most solemnly,
unless a wheat grain falls on the ground and dies,
it remains only a single grain;
but if it dies,
it yields a rich harvest.
Anyone who loves his life loses it;
anyone who hates his life in this world
will keep it for the eternal life.
If a man serves me, he must follow me,
wherever I am, my servant will be there too.
If anyone serves me, my Father will honour him.
Now my soul is troubled.
What shall I say:
Father, save me from this hour?
But it was for this very reason that I have come to this
hour.
Father, glorify your name!"

63

A voice came from heaven, "I have glorified it, and I will glorify it again."

People standing by, who heard this, said it was a clap of thunder; others said, "It was an angel speaking to him." Jesus answered, "It was not for my sake that this voice came, but for yours.

"Now sentence is being passed on this world;
now the prince of this world is to be overthrown.
And when I am lifted up from the earth,
I shall draw all men to myself."
By these words he indicated the kind of death he would die.

This is the Gospel of the Lord.

Passion Sunday

Palm Sunday

The following Gospel is read at the procession.

Gospel   Mk 11 :1–10
Blessings on him who comes in the name of the Lord.

When they were approaching Jerusalem, in sight of Bethphage and Bethany, close by the Mount of Olives, Jesus sent two of his disciples and said to them, "Go off to the village facing you, and as soon as you enter it you will find a tethered colt that no one has yet ridden. Untie it and bring it here. If anyone says to you, 'What are you doing?' say, 'The Master needs it and will send it back here directly.' "They went off and found a colt tethered near a door in the open street. As they untied it, some men standing there said, "What are you doing, untying that colt?" They gave the answer Jesus had told them, and the men let them go. Then they took the colt to Jesus and threw their cloaks on its back, and he sat on it. Many people spread their cloaks on the road, others greenery which they had cut in the fields. And those who went in front and those who followed were all shouting, "Hosanna! Blessings on him who comes in the name of the Lord! Blessings on the coming kingdom of our father David! Hosanna in the highest heavens!"

This is the Gospel of the Lord.

Alternative Gospel Jn 12:12–16
Blessings on him who comes in the name of the Lord.

The next day the crowds who had come up for the festival heard that Jesus was on his way to Jerusalem. They took branches of palm and went out to meet him, shouting, "Hosanna! Blessings on the King of Israel, who comes in the name of the Lord." Jesus found a young donkey and mounted it—as scripture says: Do not be afraid, daughter of Zion; see, your king is coming, mounted on the colt of a donkey. At the time his disciples did not understand this, but later, after Jesus had been glorified, they remembered that this had been written about him and that this was in fact how they had received him.

This is the Gospel of the Lord.

The Mass

First Reading Isaiah 50:4–7
I did not cover my face against insult—I know I shall not be shamed.

The Lord has given me
a disciple's tongue.

So that I may know how to reply to the wearied
he provides me with speech.
Each morning he wakes me to hear,
to listen like a disciple.
The Lord has opened my ear.
For my part, I made no resistance,
neither did I turn away.
I offered my back to those who struck me,
my cheeks to those who tore at my beard;
I did not cover my face
against insult and spittle.
The Lord comes to my help,
so that I am untouched by the insults.
So, too, I set my face like flint;
I know I shall not be shamed.
  This is the word of the Lord.

Responsorial Psalm Ps 21 :8–9 . 17–20 . 23–24. *R. v.* 2

1. All who see me deride me.
They curl their lips, they toss their heads.
"He trusted in the Lord, let him save him;
let him release him if this is his friend."

   Response
   My God, my God, why have you forsaken me ?

2. Many dogs have surrounded me,
a band of the wicked beset me.
They tear holes in my hands and my feet
I can count every one of my bones. (*R.*)

3. They divide my clothing among them.
They cast lots for my robe.
O Lord, do not leave me alone,
my strength, make haste to help me ! (*R.*)

4. I will tell of your name to my brethren
and praise you where they are assembled.
"You who fear the Lord give him praise;
all sons of Jacob, give him glory.
Revere him, Israel's sons." (R.)

Second Reading   Phil 2:6—11
He humbled himself, but God raised him high.

His state was divine,
yet Christ Jesus did not cling
to his equality with God
but emptied himself
to assume the condition of a slave,
and became as men are;
and being as all men are,
he was humbler yet,
even to accepting death,
death on a cross.
But God raised him high
and gave him the name
which is above all other names
so that all beings
in the heavens, on earth and in the underworld,
should bend the knee at the name of Jesus
and that every tongue should acclaim
Jesus Christ as Lord,
to the glory of God the Father.
  This is the word of the Lord.

Acclamation   Phil 2:8—9

Christ was humbler yet,
even to accepting death,
death on a cross.

But God raised him high
and gave him the name
which is above all names.

The passion of our Lord Jesus Christ

Gospel   Mk 14:1–15:47

It was two days before the Passover and the feast of
Unleavened Bread, and the chief priests and the scribes
were looking for a way to arrest Jesus by some trick
and have him put to death. For they said, "It must not
be during the festivities, or there will be a disturbance
among the people."

Jesus was at Bethany in the house of Simon the
leper; he was at dinner when a woman came in with
an alabaster jar of very costly ointment, pure nard. She
broke the jar and poured the ointment on his head.
Some who were there said to one another indignantly,
"Why this waste of ointment? Ointment like this could
have been sold for over three hundred denarii and the
money given to the poor"; and they were angry with
her. But Jesus said, "Leave her alone. Why are you
upsetting her? What she has done for me is one of the
good works. You have the poor with you always, and
you can be kind to them whenever you wish, but you
will not always have me. She has done what was in her
power to do: she has anointed my body beforehand
for its burial. I tell you solemnly, wherever throughout all the world the Good News is proclaimed, what
she has done will be told also, in remembrance of her."

Judas Iscariot, one of the Twelve, approached the
chief priests with an offer to hand Jesus over to them.
They were delighted to hear it, and promised to give
him money; and he looked for a way of betraying him
when the opportunity should occur.

On the first day of Unleavened Bread, when the Passover lamb was sacrificed, his disciples said to him, "Where do you want us to go and make the preparations for you to eat the passover?" So he sent two of his disciples, saying to them, "Go into the city and you will meet a man carrying a pitcher of water. Follow him, and say to the owner of the house which he enters, 'The Master says: Where is my dining room in which I can eat the passover with my disciples?' He will show you a large upper room furnished with couches, all prepared. Make the preparations for us there." The disciples set out and went to the city and found everything as he had told them, and prepared the Passover.

When evening came he arrived with the Twelve. And while they were at table eating, Jesus said, "I tell you solemnly, one of you is about to betray me, one of you eating with me." They were distressed and asked him, one after another, "Not I, surely?" He said to them, "It is one of the Twelve, one who is dipping into the same dish with me. Yes, the Son of Man is going to his fate, as the scriptures say he will, but alas for that man by whom the Son of Man is betrayed! Better for that man if he had never been born!"

And as they were eating he took some bread, and when he had said the blessing he broke it and gave it to them. "Take it," he said, "this is my body." Then he took a cup, and when he had returned thanks he gave it to them, and all drank from it, and he said to them, "This is my blood, the blood of the covenant, which is to be poured out for many. I tell you solemnly, I shall not drink any more wine until the day I drink the new wine in the kingdom of God."

After psalms had been sung they left for the Mount of Olives. And Jesus said to them, "You will all lose faith, for the scripture says: I shall strike the shepherd and the sheep will be scattered. However after my

resurrection I shall go before you to Galilee." Peter
said, "Even if all lose faith, I will not." And Jesus said
to him, "I tell you solemnly, this day, this very night,
before the cock crows twice, you will have disowned
me three times." But he repeated still more earnestly
"If I have to die with you, I will never disown you."
And they all said the same.

They came to a small estate called Gethsemane, and
Jesus said to his disciples, "Stay here while I pray."
Then he took Peter and James and John with him.
And a sudden fear came over him, and great distress.
And he said to them, "My soul is sorrowful to the point
of death. Wait here, and keep awake." And going on a
little further he threw himself on the ground and prayed
that, if it were possible, this hour might pass him by.
"Abba (Father)!" he said "Everything is possible for
you. Take this cup away from me. But let it be as you,
not I, would have it." He came back and found them
sleeping, and he said to Peter, "Simon, are you asleep?
Had you not the strength to keep awake one hour?
You should be awake, and praying not to be put to the
test. The spirit is willing, but the flesh is weak." Again
he went away and prayed, saying the same words.
And once more he came back and found them sleeping, their eyes were so heavy; and they could find no
answer for him. He came back a third time and said to
them, "You can sleep on now and take your rest. It is
all over. The hour has come. Now the Son of Man is
to be betrayed into the hands of sinners. Get up! Let
us go! My betrayer is close at hand already."

Even while he was still speaking, Judas, one of the
Twelve, came up with a number of men armed with
swords and clubs, sent by the chief priests and the
scribes and the elders. Now the traitor had arranged a
signal with them. "The one I kiss," he had said "he is
the man. Take him in charge, and see he is well guarded
when you lead him away." So when the traitor came,

he went straight up to Jesus and said, "Rabbi!" and kissed him. The others seized him and took him in charge. Then one of the bystanders drew his sword and struck out at the high priest's servant, and cut off his ear.

Then Jesus spoke, "Am I a brigand" he said "that you had to set out to capture me with swords and clubs? I was among you teaching in the Temple day after day and you never laid hands on me. But this is to fulfil the scriptures." And they all deserted him and ran away. A young man who followed him had nothing on but a linen cloth. They caught hold of him, but he left the cloth in their hands and ran away naked.

They led Jesus off to the high priest; and all the chief priests and the elders and the scribes assembled there. Peter had followed him at a distance, right into the high priest's palace, and was sitting with the attendants warming himself at the fire.

The chief priests and the whole Sanhedrin were looking for evidence against Jesus on which they might pass the death-sentence. But they could not find any. Several, indeed, brought false evidence against him, but their evidence was conflicting. Some stood up and submitted this false evidence against him, "We heard him say, 'I am going to destroy this Temple made by human hands, and in three days build another, not made by human hands.' " But even on this point their evidence was conflicting. The high priest then stood up before the whole assembly and put this question to Jesus, "Have you no answer to that? What is this evidence these man are bringing against you?" But he was silent and made no answer at all. The high priest put a second question to him, "Are you the Christ," he said "the Son of the Blessed One?" "I am," said Jesus "and you will see the Son of Man seated at the right hand of the Power and coming with the clouds of heaven." The high priest tore his robes, "What need of witnesses have we now?" he

said. "You heard the blasphemy. What is your finding?"
And they all gave their verdict: he deserved to die.

Some of them started spitting at him and, blind-
folding him, began hitting him with their fists and
shouting, "Play the prophet!" And the attendants
rained blows on him.

While Peter was down below in the courtyard, one
of the high priest's servant-girls came up. She saw
Peter warming himself there, stared at him and said,
"You too were with Jesus, the man from Nazareth."
But he denied it. "I do not know, I do not understand,
what you are talking about" he said. And he went out
into the forecourt. The servant-girl saw him and again
started telling the bystanders, "This fellow is one of
them." But again he denied it. A little later the bystanders themselves said to Peter, "You are one of
them for sure! Why, you are a Galilean." But he started
calling curses on himself and swearing, "I do not know
the man you speak of." At that moment the cock crew
for the second time, and Peter recalled how Jesus had
said to him, "Before the cock crows twice, you will
have disowned me three times." And he burst into
tears.

First thing in the morning, the chief priests together
with the elders and scribes, in short the whole Sanhedrin, had their plan ready. They had Jesus bound
and took him away and handed him over to Pilate.

Pilate questioned him, "Are you the king of the
Jews?" "It is you who say it" he answered. And the
chief priests brought many accusations against him.
Pilate questioned him again, "Have you no reply at all?
See how many accusations they are bringing against
you!" But, to Pilate's amazement, Jesus made no
further reply.

At festival time Pilate used to release a prisoner for
them, anyone they asked for. Now a man called
Barabbas was then in prison with the rioters who had

committed murder during the uprising. When the crowd went up and began to ask Pilate the customary favour, Pilate answered them, "Do you want me to release for you the king of the Jews?" For he realised it was out of jealousy that the chief priests had handed Jesus over. The chief priests, however, had incited the crowd to demand that he should release Barabbas for them instead. Then Pilate spoke again. "But in that case," he said to them "what am I to do with the man you call the king of the Jews?" They shouted back, "Crucify him!" "Why?" Pilate asked them "What harm has he done?" But they shouted all the louder, "Crucify him!" So Pilate, anxious to placate the crowd, released Barabbas for them and, having ordered Jesus to be scourged, handed him over to be crucified.

The soldiers led him away to the inner part of the palace, that is, the Praetorium, and called the whole cohort together. They dressed him up in purple, twisted some thorns into a crown and put it on him. And they began saluting him, "Hail, king of the Jews!" They struck his head with a reed and spat on him; and they went down on their knees to do him homage. And when they had finished making fun of him, they took off the purple and dressed him in his own clothes.

They led him out to crucify him. They enlisted a passer-by, Simon of Cyrene, father of Alexander and Rufus, who was coming in from the country, to carry his cross. They brought Jesus to the place called Golgotha, which means the place of the skull.

They offered him wine mixed with myrrh, but he refused it. Then they crucified him, and shared out his clothing, casting lots to decide what each should get. It was the third hour when they crucified him. The inscription giving the charge against him read: "The King of the Jews". And they crucified two robbers with him, one on his right and one on his left.

The passers-by jeered at him; they shook their heads

and said, "Aha! So you would destroy the temple and
rebuild it in three days! Then save yourself: come
down from the cross!" The chief priests and the
scribes mocked him among themselves in the same
way. "He saved others," they said "he cannot save himself. Let the Christ, the king of Israel, come down from
the cross now, for us to see it and believe." Even those
who were crucified with him taunted him.

When the sixth hour came there was darkness over
the whole land until the ninth hour. And at the ninth
hour Jesus cried out in a loud voice, "Eloi, Eloi, lama
sabachthani?" which means, "My God, my God, why
have you deserted me?" When some of those who
stood by heard this, they said, "Listen, he is calling on
Elijah." Someone ran and soaked a sponge in vinegar
and, putting it on a reed, gave it to him to drink saying,
"Wait and see if Elijah will come to take him down".
But Jesus gave a loud cry and breathed his last. And
the veil of the Temple was torn in two from top to
bottom. The centurion, who was standing in front of
him, had seen how he had died, and he said, "In truth
this man was a son of God".

There were some women watching from a distance.
Among them were Mary of Magdala, Mary who was
the mother of James the younger and Joset, and
Salome. These used to follow him and look after him
when he was in Galilee. And there were many other
women there who had come up to Jerusalem with
him.

It was now evening, and since it was Preparation
Day (that is, the vigil of the sabbath), there came
Joseph of Arimathaea, a prominent member of the
Council, who himself lived in the hope of seeing the
kingdom of God, and he boldly went to Pilate and
asked for the body of Jesus. Pilate, astonished that
he should have died so soon, summoned the centurion
and enquired if he was already dead. Having been

assured of this by the centurion, he granted the corpse to Joseph who bought a shroud, took Jesus down from the cross, wrapped him in the shroud and laid him in a tomb which had been hewn out of the rock. He then rolled a stone against the entrance to the. tomb. Mary of Magdala and Mary the mother of Joset were watching and took note of where he was laid.

This is the Gospel of the Lord.

Easter Sunday

The Mass of Easter Night

First Reading   Rom 6 :3–11
Christ, having been raised from the dead, will never die again.

You have been taught that when we were baptised in Christ Jesus we were baptised in his death; in other words, when we were baptised we went into the tomb with him and joined him in death, so that as Christ was raised from the dead by the Father's glory, we too might live a new life.

If in union with Christ we have imitated his death, we shall also imitate him in his resurrection. We must realise that our former selves have been crucified with him to destroy this sinful body and to free us from the slavery of sin. When a man dies, of course, he has finished with sin.

But we believe that having died with Christ we shall return to life with him : Christ, as we know, having been raised from the dead will never die again. Death has no power over him any more. When he died, he died, once for all, to sin, so his life now is life with God; and in that way, you too must consider yourselves to be dead to sin but alive for God in Christ Jesus.

This is the word of the Lord.

Responsorial Psalm   Ps 117:1–2.16–17.22–23

1. Alleluia!
Give thanks to the Lord for he is good,
for his love has no end.
Let the sons of Israel say:
"His love has no end."

   Response
   Alleluia, alleluia, alleluia!

2. The Lord's right hand has triumphed:
his right hand raised me up.
I shall not die, I shall live
and recount his deeds. (*R.*)

3. The stone which the builders rejected
has become the corner stone.
This is the work of the Lord,
a marvel in our eyes. (*R.*)

Gospel   Mk 16:1–8
Jesus of Nazareth, who was crucified, has risen.

When the sabbath was over, Mary of Magdala, Mary the mother of James, and Salome, bought spices with which to go and anoint him. And very early in the morning on the first day of the week they went to the tomb, just as the sun was rising.

They had been saying to one another, "Who will roll away the stone for us from the entrance to the tomb?" But when they looked they could see that the stone—which was very big—had already been rolled back. On entering the tomb they saw a young man in a white robe seated on the right-hand side, and they were struck with amazement. But he said to them, "There is no need for alarm. You are looking for Jesus of Nazareth, who was crucified: he has risen, he is not here. See, here is the place where they laid him. But you must go and tell his disciples and Peter, 'He is going before you to Galilee; it is there you will see him, just as he told you.' " And the women came out and ran away from the tomb because they were frightened out of their wits; and they said nothing to a soul, for they were afraid.

This is the Gospel of the Lord.

Easter Sunday

Morning Mass

First Reading   Acts 10:34.37–43
We have eaten and drunk with him after his resurrection.

Peter addressed them: "You must have heard about the recent happenings in Judaea; about Jesus of Nazareth and how he began in Galilee, after John had been preaching baptism. God had anointed him with the Holy Spirit and with power, and because God was with him, Jesus went about doing good and curing all who had fallen into the power of the devil. Now I, and those with me, can witness to everything he did throughout the countryside of Judaea and in Jerusalem itself: and also to the fact that they killed him by hanging him on a tree, yet three days afterwards God raised him to life and allowed him to be seen, not by the whole people but only by certain witnesses God had chosen beforehand. Now we are those witnesses —we have eaten and drunk with him after his resurrection from the dead—and he has ordered us to proclaim this to his people and to tell them that God has appointed him to judge everyone alive or dead. It is to him that all the prophets bear this witness: that all who believe in Jesus will have their sins forgiven through his name."

This is the word of the Lord.

Responsorial Psalm   Ps 117:1–2.16–17.22–23.
R. v. 24

1. Alleluia!
Give thanks to the Lord for he is good,
for his love has no end.
Let the sons of Israel say:
"His love has no end."

Response
This day was made by the Lord:
we rejoice and are glad.

Alternative Response
Alleluia!

2. The Lord's right hand has triumphed:
his right hand raised me up.
I shall not die, I shall live
and recount his deeds. (*R*.)

3. The stone which the builders rejected
has become the corner stone.
This is the work of the Lord,
a marvel in our eyes. (*R*.)

Second Reading   Col 3:1—4

You must look for the things that are in heaven, where Christ is.

Since you have been brought back to true life with Christ, you must look for the things that are in heaven, where Christ is, sitting at God's right hand. Let your thoughts be on heavenly things, not on the things that are on the earth, because you have died, and now the life you have is hidden with Christ in God. But when Christ is revealed—and he is your life—you too will be revealed in all your glory with him.

This is the word of the Lord.

Sequence

Christians, to the Paschal Victim offer sacrifice and
    praise.
The sheep are ransomed by the Lamb;
and Christ, the undefiled,
hath sinners to his Father reconciled.
Death with life contended: combat strangely ended!
Life's own Champion, slain, yet lives to reign.
Tell us, Mary: say what thou didst see upon the way.
The tomb the Living did enclose;
I saw Christ's glory as he rose!
The angels there attesting;
shroud with grave-clothes resting.
Christ, my hope, has risen: he goes before you into
    Galilee.
That Christ is truly risen from the dead we know.
Victorious king, thy mercy show!
Amen. Alleluia!

Alleluia   1 Cor 5:7–8

Alleluia, alleluia!
Christ, our passover, has been sacrificed;
let us celebrate the feast then, in the Lord.
Alleluia!

Gospel   Jn 20:1–9
He must rise from the dead.

It was very early on the first day of the week and still dark, when Mary of Magdala came to the tomb. She saw that the stone had been moved away from the tomb and came running to Simon Peter and the other disciple, the one Jesus loved. "They have taken the Lord out of the tomb" she said "and we don't know where they have put him."

So Peter set out with the other disciple to go to the tomb. They ran together, but the other disciple, running faster than Peter, reached the tomb first; he bent down and saw the linen cloths lying on the ground, but did not go in. Simon Peter who was following now came up, went right into the tomb, saw the linen cloths on the ground, and also the cloth that had been over his head; this was not with the linen cloths but rolled up in a place by itself. Then the other disciple who had reached the tomb first also went in; he saw and he believed. Till this moment they had failed to understand the teaching of scripture, that he must rise from the dead.

This is the Gospel of the Lord...

2nd Sunday of Easter

First Reading   Acts 4:32–35
United, heart and soul.

The whole group of believers was united, heart and
soul; no one claimed for his own use anything that
he had, as everything they owned was held in
common.

The apostles continued to testify to the resurrection
of the Lord Jesus with great power, and they were all
given great respect.

None of their members was ever in want, as all those
who owned land or houses would sell them, and bring
the money from them, to present it to the apostles; it
it was then distributed to any members who might be in
need.

This is the word of the Lord.

Responsorial Psalm   Ps 117:2–4.15–18.22–24.
                                                              R. v. 1

1. Let the sons of Israel say:
"His love has no end."
Let the sons of Aaron say:
"His love has no end."
Let those who fear the Lord say:
"His love has no end."

   Response
   Give thanks to the Lord for he is good,
   for his love has no end.

   Alternative Response
   Alleluia!

2. The Lord's right hand has triumphed;
his right hand raised me up.
I shall not die, I shall live
and recount his deeds.
I was punished, I was punished by the Lord,
but not doomed to die. (*R.*)

3. The stone which the builders rejected
has become the corner stone.
This is the work of the Lord,
a marvel in our eyes.
This day was made by the Lord;
we rejoice and are glad. (*R.*)

Second Reading   1 Jn 5 :1–6
*Anyone who has been begotten by God has already
overcome the world.*

Whoever believes that Jesus is the Christ
has been begotten by God;
and whoever loves the Father that begot him
loves the child whom he begets.
We can be sure that we love God's children
if we love God himself and do what he has commanded
    us;
this is what loving God is—
keeping his commandments;
and his commandments are not difficult,
because anyone who has been begotten by God
has already overcome the world;
this is the victory over the world—
our faith.
Who can overcome the world?
Only the man who believes that Jesus is the Son of
    God;

Jesus Christ who came by water and blood,
not with water only,
but with water and blood;
with the Spirit as another witness—
since the Spirit is the truth.
    This is the word of the Lord.

Alleluia   Jn 20:29

Alleluia, alleluia!
Jesus said: "You believe because you can see me.
Happy are those who have not seen and yet believe."
Alleluia!

Gospel   Jn 20:19–31
Eight days later, Jesus came.

In the evening of that same day, the first day of the
week, the doors were closed in the room where the
disciples were, for fear of the Jews. Jesus came and
stood among them. He said to them, "Peace be with
you," and showed them this hands and his side. The
disciples were filled with joy when they saw the Lord,
and he said to them again, "Peace be with you.
"As the Father sent me,
so am I sending you."
After saying this he breathed on them and said:
"Receive the Holy Spirit.
For those whose sins you forgive,
they are forgiven;
for those whose sins you retain,
they are retained."
    Thomas, called the Twin, who was one of the Twelve,
was not with them when Jesus came. When the disciples
said, "We have seen the Lord", he answered, "Unless I

see the holes that the nails made in his hands and can put my finger into the holes they made, and unless I can put my hand into his side, I refuse to believe." Eight days later the disciples were in the house again and Thomas was with them. The doors were closed, but Jesus came in and stood among them. "Peace be with you" he said. Then he spoke to Thomas, "Put your finger here; look, here are my hands. Give me your hand; put it into my side. Doubt no longer but believe." Thomas replied, "My Lord and my God!" Jesus said to him:
"You believe because you can see me.
Happy are those who have not seen and yet believe."

There were many other signs that Jesus worked and the disciples saw, but they are not recorded in this book. These are recorded so that you may believe that Jesus is the Christ, the Son of God, and that believing this you may have life through his name.

This is the Gospel of the Lord.

3rd Sunday of Easter

First Reading Acts 3:13–15.17–19
You killed the prince of life. God, however, raised him from the dead.

Peter said to the people: "You are Israelites, and it is the God of Abraham, Isaac and Jacob, the God of our ancestors, who has glorified his servant Jesus, the same Jesus you handed over and then disowned in the presence of Pilate, after Pilate had decided to release him. It was you who accused the Holy One, the Just One, you who demanded the reprieve of a murderer while you killed the prince of life. God, however, raised him from the dead, and to that fact we are the witnesses.

"Now I know, brothers, that neither you nor your leaders had any idea what you were really doing; this was the way God carried out what he had foretold, when he said through all his prophets that his Christ would suffer. Now you must repent and turn to God, so that your sins may be wiped out."

This is the word of the Lord.

Responsorial Psalm
Ps 4:2.4.7.9 *R. v.* 7

1. When I call, answer me, O God of justice;
from anguish you released me, have mercy and hear me!

Response
Lift up the light of your face on us, O Lord.

Alternative Response
Alleluia!

2. It is the Lord who grants favours to those whom he loves;
the Lord hears me whenever I call him. (*R.*)

3. "What can bring us happiness?" many say.
Lift up the light of your face on us, O Lord. (*R.*)

4. I will lie down in peace and sleep comes at once,
for you alone, Lord, make me dwell in safety. (*R.*)

Second Reading
1 Jn 2:1–5
He is the sacrifice that takes our sins away, and not only ours, but the whole world's.

I am writing this, my children,
to stop you sinning;

85

but if anyone should sin,
we have our advocate with the Father,
Jesus Christ, who is just;
he is the sacrifice that takes our sins away,
and not only ours,
but the whole world's.
We can be sure that we know God
only by keeping his commandments.
Anyone who says, "I know him",
and does not keep his commandments,
is a liar,
refusing to admit the truth.
But when anyone does obey what he has said,
God's love comes to perfection in him.
   This is the word of the Lord.

Alleluia   Cf. Lk 24:32

Alleluia, alleluia!
Lord Jesus, explain the scriptures to us.
Make our hearts burn within us
as you talk to us.
Alleluia!

Gospel   Lk 24:35–48
*So you see how it is written that the Christ would suffer
and on the third day rise from the dead.*

The disciples told their story of what had happened
on the road and how they had recognised Jesus at the
breaking of bread.
   They were still talking about all this when Jesus
himself stood among them and said to them, "Peace
be with you!" In a state of alarm and fright, they
thought they were seeing a ghost. But he said, "Why
86

are you so agitated, and why are these doubts rising in your hearts? Look at my hands and feet; yes, it is I indeed. Touch me and see for yourselves; a ghost has no flesh and bones as you can see I have." And as he said this he showed them his hands and feet. Their joy was so great that they could not believe it, and they stood dumbfounded; so he said to them, "Have you anything here to eat?" And they offered him a piece of grilled fish, which he took and ate before their eyes.

Then he told them, "This is what I meant when I said, while I was still with you, that everything written about me in the Law of Moses, in the Prophets and in the Psalms, has to be fulfilled." He then opened their minds to understand the scriptures, and he said to them, "So you see how it is written that the Christ would suffer and on the third day rise from the dead, and that, in his name, repentance for the forgiveness of sins would be preached to all the nations, beginning from Jerusalem. You are witnesses to this."

This is the Gospel of the Lord.

4th Sunday of Easter

First Reading   Acts 4:8–12
This is the only name by which we can be saved.

Peter, filled with the Holy Spirit, addressed them, "Rulers of the people, and elders! If you are questioning us today about an act of kindness to a cripple, and asking us how he was healed, then I am glad to tell you all, and would indeed be glad to tell the whole people of Israel, that it was by the name of Jesus Christ the Nazarene, the one you crucified, whom God raised from the dead, by this name and by no other that this man is able to stand up perfectly healthy, here in your presence, today. This is the stone rejected by you the builders, but which has proved to be the keystone. For of all the names in the world given to men, this is the only one by which we can be saved."

This is the word of the Lord.

Responsorial Psalm Ps 117:1.8–9.21–23.26.28–29.

R. v. 22

1. Alleluia!
Give thanks to the Lord for he is good,
for his love has no end.
It is better to take refuge in the Lord
than to trust in men:
it is better to take refuge in the Lord
than to trust in princes.

Response
The stone which the builders rejected
has become the corner stone.

Alternative Response
Alleluia!

2. I will thank you for you have given answer
and you are my saviour.
The stone which the builders rejected
has become the corner stone.
This is the work of the Lord,
a marvel in our eyes. (*R.*)

3. Blessed in the name of the Lord
is he who comes.
We bless you from the house of the Lord;
I will thank you for you have given answer
and you are my saviour.
Give thanks to the Lord for he is good;
for his love has no end. (*R.*)

Second Reading 1 Jn 3 : 1–2
We shall see God as he really is.

Think of the love that the Father has lavished on us,
by letting us be called God's children;
and that is what we are.
Because the world refused to acknowledge him,
therefore it does not acknowledge us.
My dear people, we are already the children of God
but what we are to be in the future has not yet been
   revealed;
all we know is, that when it is revealed
we shall be like him
because we shall see him as he really is.
   This is the word of the Lord.

Alleluia Jn 10 : 14

Alleluia, alleluia!
I am the good shepherd, says the Lord;
I know my own sheep and my own know me.
Alleluia!

Gospel Jn 10 : 11–18
*The good shepherd is one who lays down his life for his
sheep.*

Jesus said:
"I am the good shepherd:
the good shepherd is one who lays down his life for
   his sheep.
The hired man, since he is not the shepherd
and the sheep do not belong to him,
abandons the sheep and runs away

as soon as he sees a wolf coming,
and then the wolf attacks and scatters the sheep :
this is because he is only a hired man
and has no concern for the sheep.
I am the good shepherd ;
I know my own
and my own know me,
just as the Father knows me
and I know the Father ;
and I lay down my life for my sheep.
And there are other sheep I have
that are not of this fold,
and these I have to lead as well.
They too will listen to my voice,
and there will be only one flock,
and one shepherd.
The Father loves me,
because I lay down my life
in order to take it up again.
No one takes it from me ;
I lay it down of my own free will,
and as it is in my power to lay it down,
so it is in my power to take it up again ;
and this is the command I have been given by my Father."
This is the Gospel of the Lord.

5th Sunday of Easter

First Reading   Acts 9 :26–31

*Barnabas explained how the Lord had appeared to Saul
on his journey.*

When Saul got to Jerusalem he tried to join the disciples, but they were afraid of him : they could not

believe he was really a disciple. Barnabas, however, took charge of him, introduced him to the apostles, and explained how the Lord had appeared to Saul and spoken to him on his journey, and how he had preached boldly at Damascus in the name of Jesus. Saul now started to go round with them in Jerusalem, preaching fearlessly in the name of the Lord. But after he had spoken to the Hellenists, and argued with them, they became determined to kill him. When the brothers knew, they took him to Caesarea, and sent him off from there to Tarsus.

The churches throughout Judaea, Galilee and Samaria were now left in peace, building themselves up, living in the fear of the Lord, and filled with the consolation of the Holy Spirit.

This is the word of the Lord.

Responsorial Psalm   Ps 21:26–28. 30–32. *R.* v. 26

1. My vows I will pay before those who fear him.
The poor shall eat and shall have their fill.
They shall praise the Lord, those who seek him.
May their hearts live for ever and ever !

Response
You, Lord, are my praise in the great assembly.

Alternative Response
Alleluia !

2. All the earth shall remember and return to the Lord,
all families of the nations worship before him.
They shall worship him, all the mighty of the earth ;
before him shall bow all who go down to the dust. (*R.*)

3. And my soul shall live for him, my children serve
   him.
They shall tell of the Lord to generations yet to come,
declare his faithfulness to peoples yet unborn:
"These things the Lord has done." (R.)

Second Reading   1 Jn 3:18–24
His commandments are these: that we believe in his Son
and that we love one another.

My children,
our love is not to be just words or mere talk,
but something real and active;
only by this can we be certain
that we are the children of the truth
and be able to quieten our conscience in his presence,
whatever accusations it may raise against us,
because God is greater than our conscience and he
   knows everything.
My dear people,
if we cannot be condemned by our own conscience,
we need not be afraid in God's presence,
and whatever we ask him,
we shall receive,
because we keep his commandments
and live the kind of life that he wants.
His commandments are these:
that we believe in the name of his Son Jesus Christ
and that we love one another
as he told us to.
Whoever keeps his commandments
lives in God and God lives in him.
We know that he lives in us
by the Spirit that he has given us.
   This is the word of God.

Alleluia
Jn 15 :4—5

Alleluia, alleluia !
Make your home in me, as I make mine in you.
Whoever remains in me bears fruit in plenty.
Alleluia !

Gospel
Jn 15 :1—8
Whoever remains in me, with me in him, bears fruit in plenty.

Jesus said to his disciples:
"I am the true vine,
and my Father is the vinedresser.
Every branch in me that bears no fruit
he cuts away,
and every branch that does bear fruit he prunes
to make it bear even more.
You are pruned already,
by means of the word that I have spoken to you.
Make your home in me, as I make mine in you.
As a branch cannot bear fruit all by itself,
but must remain part of the vine,
neither can you unless you remain in me.
I am the vine,
you are the branches.
Whoever remains in me, with me in him,
bears fruit in plenty;
for cut off from me you can do nothing.
Anyone who does not remain in me
is like a branch that has been thrown away
—he withers;
these branches are collected and thrown on the fire,
and they are burnt.
If you remain in me

and my words remain in you,
you may ask what you will
and you shall get it.
It is to the glory of my Father that you should bear
  much fruit,
and then you will be my disciples."
  This is the Gospel of the Lord.

6th Sunday of Easter

First Reading   Acts 10:25–26.34–35.44–48
The Holy Spirit has been poured out on the pagans too.

As Peter reached the house Cornelius went out to meet
him, knelt at his feet and prostrated himself. But Peter
helped him up. "Stand up," he said "I am only a man
after all!"

  Then Peter addressed them: "The truth I have now
come to realise" he said "is that God does not have
favourites, but that anybody of any nationality who
fears God and does what is right is acceptable to him."

  While Peter was still speaking the Holy Spirit came
down on all the listeners. Jewish believers who had
accompanied Peter were all astonished that the gift
of the Holy Spirit should be poured out on the pagans
too, since they could hear them speaking strange
languages and proclaiming the greatness of God.
Peter himself then said, "Could anyone refuse the
water of baptism to these people, now they have
received the Holy Spirit just as much as we have?" He
then gave orders for them to be baptised in the name
of Jesus Christ. Afterwards they begged him to stay
on for some days.

  This is the word of the Lord.

Responsorial Psalm   Ps 97 :1–4. *R.* v. 2

1. Sing a new song to the Lord
for he has worked wonders.
His right hand and his holy arm
have brought salvation.

Response
The Lord has shown his salvation to the nations.

Alternative Response
Alleluia !

2. The Lord has made known his salvation ;
has shown his justice to the nations.
He has remembered his truth and love
for the house of Israel. (*R.*)

3. All the ends of the earth have seen
the salvation of our God.
Shout to the Lord all the earth,
ring out your joy. (*R.*)

Second Reading   1 Jn 4 :7–10
God is love.

My dear people,
let us love one another
since love comes from God
and everyone who loves is begotten by God and knows
    God.
Anyone who fails to love can never have known God,
because God is love.
God's love for us was revealed
when God sent into the world his only Son

so that we could have life through him;
this is the love I mean:
not our love for God,
but God's love for us when he sent his Son
to be the sacrifice that takes our sins away.
   This is the word of the Lord.

Alleluia

Jn 14:23

Alleluia, alleluia!
Jesus said: "If anyone loves me he will keep my word,
and my Father will love him,
and we shall come to him."
Alleluia!

Gospel

Jn 15:9–17

A man can have no greater love than to lay down his life
for his friends.

Jesus said to his disciples:
"As the Father has loved me,
so I have loved you.
Remain in my love.
If you keep my commandments
you will remain in my love,
just as I have kept my Father's commandments
and remain in his love.
I have told you this
so that my own joy may be in you
and your joy be complete.
This is my commandment:
love one another,
as I have loved you.
A man can have no greater love
than to lay down his life for his friends.

You are my friends,
if you do what I command you.
I shall not call you servants any more,
because a servant does not know
his master's business;
I call you friends,
because I have made known to you
everything I have learnt from my Father.
You did not choose me,
no, I chose you;
and I commissioned you
to go out and to bear fruit,
fruit that will last;
and then the Father will give you
anything you ask him in my name.
What I command you
is to love one another."

    This is the Gospel of the Lord.

7th Sunday of Easter

Sunday after Ascension

First Reading   Acts 1:15–17.20–26
We must choose one of these to be a witness to his resurrection with us.

One day Peter stood up to speak to the brothers—
there were about a hundred and twenty persons in the
congregation: "Brothers, the passage of scripture had
to be fulfilled in which the Holy Spirit, speaking
through David, foretells the fate of Judas, who offered
himself as a guide to the men who arrested Jesus—

after having been one of our number and actually sharing
this ministry of ours.
In the Book of Psalms it says:
Let someone else take this office.
"We must therefore choose someone who has been
with us the whole time that the Lord Jesus was
travelling round with us, someone who was with us
right from the time when John was baptising until the
day when he was taken up from us—and he can act
with us as a witness to his resurrection."

Having nominated two candidates, Joseph known
as Barsabbas, whose surname was Justus, and Matthias,
they prayed, "Lord, you can read everyone's heart;
show us therefore which of these two you have chosen
to take over this ministry and apostolate, which Judas
abandoned to go to his proper place." They then drew
lots for them, and as the lot fell to Matthias, he was
listed as one of the twelve apostles.

This is the word of the Lord.

Responsorial Psalm   Ps 102:1–2.11–12.19–20.
                                                    R. v. 19

1. My soul, give thanks to the Lord,
all my being, bless his holy name.
My soul, give thanks to the Lord
and never forget all his blessings.

   Response
   The Lord has set his sway in heaven.

   Alternative Response
   Alleluia !

2. For as the heavens are high above the earth
so strong is his love for those who fear him.
As far as the east is from the west
so far does he remove our sins. (*R.*)

3. The Lord has set his sway in heaven
and his kingdom is ruling over all.
Give thanks to the Lord, all his angels,
mighty in power, fulfilling his word. (*R.*)

Second Reading   1 Jn 4:11—16

Anyone who lives in love lives in God, and God lives in him.

My dear people,
since God has loved us so much,
we too should love one another.
No one has ever seen God;
but as long as we love one another
God will live in us
and his love will be complete in us.
We can know that we are living in him
and he is living in us
because he lets us share his Spirit.
We ourselves saw and we testify
that the Father sent his Son
as saviour of the world.
If anyone acknowledges that Jesus is the Son of God,
God lives in him, and he in God.
We ourselves have known and put our faith in
God's love towards ourselves.
God is love
and anyone who lives in love lives in God,
and God lives in him.
    This is the word of the Lord.

Alleluia   Jn 14:18

Alleluia, alleluia!
I will not leave you orphans, says the Lord;

I will come back to you,
and your hearts will be full of joy.
Alleluia!

Gospel   Jn 17:11–19
That they may be one like us!

Jesus raised his eyes to heaven and said:
"Holy Father,
keep those you have given me true to your name,
so that they may be one like us.
While I was with them,
I kept those you had given me true to your name.
I have watched over them and not one is lost
except the one who chose to be lost,
and this was to fulfil the scriptures.
But now I am coming to you
and while still in the world I say these things
to share my joy with them to the full.
I passed your word on to them,
and the world hated them,
because they belong to the world
no more than I belong to the world.
I am not asking you to remove them from the world,
but to protect them from the evil one.
They do not belong to the world
any more than I belong to the world.
Consecrate them in the truth;
your word is truth.
As you sent me into the world,
I have sent them into the world,
and for their sake I consecrate myself
so that they too may be consecrated in truth."
    This is the Gospel of the Lord.

Pentecost Sunday

First Reading   Acts 2 :1–11
They were all filled with the Holy Spirit and began to speak.

When Pentecost day came round, the apostles had all met in one room, when suddenly they heard what sounded like a powerful wind from heaven, the noise of which filled the entire house in which they were sitting ; and something appeared to them that seemed like tongues of fire ; these separated and came to rest on the head of each of them. They were all filled with the Holy Spirit, and began to speak foreign languages as the Spirit gave them the gift of speech.

Now there were devout men living in Jerusalem from every nation under heaven, and at this sound they all assembled, each one bewildered to hear these men speaking his own language. They were amazed and astonished. "Surely" they said "all these men speaking are Galileans ? How does it happen that each of us hears them in his own native language ? Parthians, Medes and Elamites ; people from Mesopotamia, Judaea and Cappadocia, Pontus and Asia, Phrygia and Pamphylia, Egypt and the parts of Libya round Cyrene ; as well as visitors from Rome—Jews and proselytes alike—Cretans and Arabs ; we hear them preaching in our own language about the marvels of God."

This is the word of the Lord.

Responsorial Psalm   Ps 103 :1 . 24 . 29–31 . 34. *R.* v. 30

1. Bless the Lord, my soul !
Lord God, how great you are,

How many are your works, O Lord!
The earth is full of your riches.

Response
Send forth your Spirit, O Lord,
and renew the face of the earth.

Alternative Response
Alleluia!

2. You take back your spirit, they die,
returning to the dust from which they came.
You send forth your spirit, they are created;
and you renew the face of the earth. (*R.*)

3. May the glory of the Lord last for ever!
May the Lord rejoice in his works!
May my thoughts be pleasing to him.
I find my joy in the Lord. (*R.*)

Second Reading   1 Cor 12:3–7.12–13
In the one Spirit we were all baptised.

No one can say, "Jesus is our Lord" unless he is under the
influence of the Holy Spirit.

There is a variety of gifts but always the same Spirit;
there are all sorts of service to be done, but always to
the same Lord; working in all sorts of different ways
in different people, it is the same God who is working
in all of them. The particular way in which the Spirit
is given to each person is for a good purpose.

Just as a human body, though it is made up of many
parts, is a single unit because all these parts, though
many, make one body, so it is with Christ. In the one
Spirit we were all baptised, Jews as well as Greeks,
slaves as well as citizens, and one Spirit was given to
us all to drink.

This is the word of the Lord.

Sequence &

Alleluia

Alleluia, allelluia!
Come, Holy Spirit, fill the hearts of your faithful,
and kindle in them the fire of your love.
Alleluia!

Gospel   Jn 20:19–23

As the Father sent me, so am I sending you: receive the Holy Spirit.

In the evening of that same day, the first day of the week, the doors were closed in the room where the disciples were, for fear of the Jews. Jesus came and stood among them. He said to them, "Peace be with you," and showed them his hands and his side. The disciples were filled with joy when they saw the Lord, and he said to them again. "Peace be with you.
"As the Father sent me,
so am I sending you."
After saying this he breathed on them and said:
"Receive the Holy Spirit
For those whose sins you forgive,
they are forgiven;
for those whose sins you retain,
they are retained."
   This is the Gospel of the Lord.

Sunday after Pentecost

The Holy Trinity

First Reading   Deut 4:32–34.39–40
*The Lord is God indeed, in heaven above as on earth
beneath, he and no other.*

Moses said to the people: "Put this question, then, to
the ages that are past, that went before you, from the
time God created man on earth: Was there ever a word
so majestic, from one end of heaven to the other? Was
anything ever heard? Did ever a people hear the voice
of the living God speaking from the heart of the fire,
as you heard it, and remain alive? Has any god
ventured to take to himself one nation from the midst
of another by ordeals, signs, wonders, war with mighty
hand and outstretched arm, by fearsome terrors—all this that
the Lord your God did for you before your eyes in Egypt?

"Understand this today, therefore, and take it to
heart: The Lord is God indeed, in heaven above as on
earth beneath, he and no other. Keep his laws and
commandments as I give them to you today, so that
you and your children may prosper and live long in the
land that the Lord your God gives you for ever."

This is the word of the Lord.

Responsorial Psalm   Ps 32:4–6.9.18–20.22.
                                        R. v. 12

1. The word of the Lord is faithful
and all his works to be trusted.
The Lord loves justice and right
and fills the earth with his love.

Response
Happy the people the Lord has chosen as his own.

2. By his word the heavens were made,
by the breath of his mouth all the stars.
He spoke ; and it came to be.
He commanded ; it sprang into being. (*R.*)

3. The Lord looks on those who revere him,
on those who hope in his love,
to rescue their souls from death,
to keep them alive in famine. (*R.*)

4. Our soul is waiting for the Lord.
The Lord is our help and our shield.
May your love be upon us, O Lord.
as we place all our hope in you. (*R.*)

Second Reading   Rom 8 :14–17
*You received the spirit of sons, and it makes us cry out,
"Abba, Father!"*

Everyone moved by the Spirit is a son of God. The
spirit you received is not the spirit of slaves bringing
fear into your lives again ; it is the spirit of sons, and it
makes us cry out, "Abba, Father !" The Spirit himself
and our spirit bear united witness that we are children
of God. And if we are children we are heirs as well :
heirs of God and coheirs with Christ, sharing his
suffering so as to share his glory.
    This is the word of the Lord.

Alleluia   Apoc 1 :8

Alleluia, alleluia !

Glory be to the Father, and to the Son, and to the Holy
  Spirit,
the God who is, who was, and who is to come.
Alleluia!

Gospel   Mt 28:16–20
*Baptise them in the name of the Father and of the Son
and of the Holy Spirit.*

The eleven disciples set out for Galilee, to the mountain
where Jesus had arranged to meet them. When they
saw him they fell down before him, though some
hesitated. Jesus came up and spoke to them. He said,
"All authority in heaven and on earth has been given to
me. Go, therefore, make disciples of all the nations;
baptise them in the name of the Father and of the Son
and of the Holy Spirit, and teach them to observe all
the commands I gave you. And know that I am with
you always; yes, to the end of time."
  This is the Gospel of the Lord.

6th Sunday of the Year*

First Reading   Lev 13:1–2.45–46
The leper must live apart: he must live outside the camp.

The Lord said to Moses and Aaron, "If a swelling or
scab or shiny spot appears on a man's skin, a case
of leprosy of the skin is to be suspected. The man must
be taken to Aaron, the priest, or to one of the priests
who are his sons.

*In 1970, the 6th–8th Sundays of the year are omitted.

"A man infected with leprosy must wear his clothing torn and his hair disordered; he must shield his upper lip and cry, 'Unclean, unclean'. As long as the disease lasts he must be unclean; and therefore he must live apart: he must live outside the camp."

This is the word of the Lord.

Responsorial Psalm
Ps 31 :1–2 . 5 . 11 . *R.* v. 7

1. Happy the man whose offence is forgiven,
whose sin is remitted.
O happy the man to whom the Lord
imputes no guilt,
in whose spirit is no guile.

Response
You are my hiding place, O Lord;
you surround me with cries of deliverance.

2. But now I have acknowledged my sins;
my guilt I did not hide.
I said: "I will confess
my offence to the Lord."
And you, Lord, have forgiven
the guilt of my sin. (*R.*)

3. Rejoice, rejoice in the Lord,
exult, you just!
O come, ring out your joy,
all you upright of heart. (*R.*)

Second Reading
1 Cor 10:31–11 :1
Take me for your model, as I take Christ.

Whatever you eat, whatever you drink, whatever you do at all, do it for the glory of God. Never do anything offensive to anyone—to Jews or Greeks or to the Church of God; just as I try to be helpful to everyone at all times, not anxious for my own advantage but for the advantage of everybody else, so that they may be saved.

Take me for your model, as I take Christ.

This is the word of the Lord.

Alleluia. See pp. 184–6.

Gospel Mk 1 :40–45

The leprosy left him at once and he was cured.

A leper came to Jesus and pleaded on his knees: "If you want to" he said "you can cure me." Feeling sorry for him, Jesus stretched out his hand and touched him. "Of course I want to!" he said. "Be cured!" And the leprosy left him at once and he was cured. Jesus immediately sent him away and sternly ordered him, "Mind you say nothing to anyone, but go and show yourself to the priest, and make the offering for your healing prescribed by Moses as evidence of your recovery." The man went away, but then started talking about it freely and telling the story everywhere, so that Jesus could no longer go openly into any town, but had to stay outside in places where nobody lived. Even so, people from all around would come to him.

This is the Gospel of the Lord.

7th Sunday of the Year*

First Reading   Isaiah 43:18–19.21–22.24–25
I it is who must blot out everything.

Thus says the Lord:
No need to recall the past,
no need to think about what was done before.
See, I am doing a new deed,
even now it comes to light: can you not see it?
Yes, I am making a road in the wilderness,
paths in the wilds.
The people I have formed for myself
will sing my praises.
Jacob, you have not invoked me,
you have not troubled yourself, Israel, on my behalf.
Instead you have burdened me with your sins,
troubled me with your iniquities.
I it is, who must blot out everything
and not remember your sins.
   This is the word of the Lord.

Responsorial Psalm   Ps 40:2–5.13–14. *R.* v. 5

1. Happy the man who considers the poor and the
   weak.
The Lord will save him in the day of evil.
will guard him, give him life, make him happy in the
   land
and will not give him up to the will of his foes.

---

*In 1970, the 6th–8th Sundays of the year are omitted.

Response
Heal my soul for I have sinned against you.

2. The Lord will help him on his bed of pain,
he will bring him back from sickness to health.
As for me, I said : "Lord, have mercy on me,
heal my soul for I have sinned against you." (*R.*)

3. If you uphold me I shall be unharmed
and set in your presence for evermore.
Blessed be the Lord, the God of Israel
from age to age. Amen. Amen. (*R.*)

Second Reading   2 Cor 1 :18–22
Jesus was never Yes and No: with him it was always Yes.

I swear by God's truth, there is no Yes and No about
what we say to you. The Son of God, the Christ Jesus
that we proclaimed among you—I mean Silvanus and
Timothy and I—was never Yes and No : with him it
was always Yes, and however many the promises God
made, the Yes to them all is in him. That is why it is
"through him" that we answer Amen to the praise of
God. Remember it is God himself who assures us all,
and you, of our standing in Christ, and has anointed
us, marking us with his seal and giving us the pledge,
the Spirit, that we carry in our hearts.
  This is the word of the Lord.

Alleluia.   See pp. 184–6.

Gospel   Mk 2 :1–12
The Son of Man has authority on earth to forgive sins.

When Jesus returned to Capernaum, word went round
that he was back; and so many people collected that
110

there was no room left, even in front of the door. He was preaching the word to them when some people came bringing him a paralytic carried by four men, but as the crowd made it impossible to get the man to him, they stripped the roof over the place where Jesus was; and when they had made an opening, they lowered the stretcher on which the paralytic lay. Seeing their faith, Jesus said to the paralytic, "My child, your sins are forgiven." Now some scribes were sitting there, and they thought to themselves, "How can this man talk like that? He is blaspheming. Who can forgive sins but God?" Jesus, inwardly aware that this was what they were thinking, said to them, "Why do you have these thoughts in your hearts? Which of these is easier: to say to the paralytic, 'Your sins are forgiven' or to say, 'Get up, pick up your stretcher and walk'? But to prove to you that the Son of Man has authority on earth to forgive sins," —he said to the paralytic—"I order you: get up, pick up your stretcher, and go off home." And the man got up, picked up his stretcher at once and walked out in front of everyone, so that they were all astounded and praised God saying, "We have never seen anything like this."

This is the Gospel of the Lord.

8th Sunday of the Year*

First Reading   Hosea 2:16–17. 21–22
I will betroth you to myself for ever.

Thus says the Lord:
I am going to lure her

_____
*In 1970, the 6th–8th Sundays of the year are omitted.

and lead her out into the wilderness
and speak to her heart.
There she will respond to me as she did when she was
   young,
as she did when she came out of the land of Egypt.
I will betroth you to myself for ever,
betroth you with integrity and justice,
with tenderness and love;
I will betroth you to myself with faithfulness,
and you will come to know the Lord.
   This is the word of the Lord.

Responsorial Psalm   Ps 102:1–4.8.10.12–13.
                                  R. v. 8

1. My soul, give thanks to the Lord,
all my being, bless his holy name.
My soul, give thanks to the Lord
and never forget all his blessings.

   Response
   The Lord is compassion and love.

2. It is he who forgives all your guilt,
who heals every one of your ills,
who redeems your life from the grave,
who crowns you with love and compassion. (*R*.)

3. The Lord is compassion and love,
slow to anger and rich in mercy.
He does not treat us according to our sins
nor repay us according to our faults. (*R*.)

4. As far as the east is from the west
so far does he remove our sins.
As a father has compassion on his sons,
The Lord has pity on those who fear him. (*R*.)

Second Reading   2 Cor 3 :1–6
You are a letter from Christ drawn up by us.

Unlike other people, we need no letters of recom-
mendation either to you or from you, because you are
yourselves our letter, written in our hearts, that anybody
can see and read, and it is plain that you are a letter from
Christ, drawn up by us, and written not with ink but with
the Spirit of the living God, not on stone tablets but on
the tablets of your living hearts.

Before God, we are confident of this through Christ:
not that we are qualified in ourselves to claim anything as
our own work: all our qualifications come from God. He
is the one who has given us the qualifications to be the
administrators of this new covenant, which is not a
covenant of written letters but of the Spirit: the written
letters bring death, but the Spirit gives life.

This is the word of the Lord.

Alleluia   See pp. 184–6.

Gospel   Mk 2 :18–22
The bridegroom is with them.

One day when John's disciples and the Pharisees were
fasting, some people came and said to Jesus, "Why is
it that John's disciples and the disciples of the Pharisees
fast, but your disciples do not?" Jesus replied, "Surely the
bridegroom's attendants would never think of fasting
while the bridegroom is still with them? As long as they
have the bridegroom with them, they could not think of
fasting. But the time will come for the bridegroom to be
taken away from them, and then, on that day, they will
fast. No one sews a piece of unshrunken cloth on an old
cloak; if he does, the patch pulls away from it, the new

113

from the old, and the tear gets worse. And nobody puts new wine into old wineskins; if he does, the wine will burst the skins, and the wine is lost and the skins too. No! New wine, fresh skins!"

This is the Gospel of the Lord.

9th Sunday of the Year*

First Reading Deut 5:12–15
Remember that you were a servant in the land of Egypt.

The Lord says this: "Observe the sabbath day and keep it holy, as the Lord your God has commanded you. For six days you shall labour and do all your work, but the seventh day is a sabbath for the Lord your God. You shall do no work that day, neither you nor your son nor your daughter nor your servants, men or women, nor your ox nor your donkey nor any of your animals, nor the stranger who lives with you. Thus your servant, man or woman, shall rest as you do. Remember that you were a servant in the land of Egypt, and that the Lord your God brought you out from there with mighty hand and outstretched arm; because of this, the Lord your God has commanded you to keep the sabbath day."

This is the word of the Lord.

Responsorial Psalm Ps 80:3–8.10–11. R. v. 2

1. Raise a song and sound the timbrel,
the sweet-sounding harp and the lute,

---

*In 1970, the 9th Sunday of the Year falls on 31 May, and follows the Sunday after Pentecost, Feast of the Holy Trinity.

blow the trumpet at the new moon,
when the moon is full, on our feast.

Response
Ring out your joy to God our strength.

2. For this is Israel's law,
a command of the God of Jacob.
He imposed it as a rule on Joseph,
when he went out against the land of Egypt. (*R.*)

3. A voice I did not know said to me:
"I freed your shoulder from the burden;
your hands were freed from the load.
You called in distress and I saved you. (*R.*)

4. "Let there be no foreign god among you,
no worship of an alien god.
I am the Lord your God,
who brought you from the land of Egypt.' (*R.*)

Second Reading   2 Cor 4:6–11
In our mortal flesh the life of Jesus is openly shown.

It is the same God that said, "Let there be light shining
out of darkness," who has shone in our minds to radiate
the light of the knowledge of God's glory, the glory on the
face of Christ.

We are only the earthenware jars that hold this treasure,
to make it clear that such an overwhelming power comes
from God and not from us. We are in difficulties on all
sides, but never cornered; we see no answer to our
problems, but never despair; we have been persecuted,
but never deserted; knocked down, but never killed;
always, wherever we may be, we carry with us in our body
the death of Jesus, so that the life of Jesus, too, may

115

always be seen in our body. Indeed, while we are still alive, we are consigned to our death every day, for the sake of Jesus, so that in our mortal flesh the life of Jesus, too, may be openly shown.

This is the word of the Lord.

Alleluia See pp. 184–6.

Gospel Mk 2:23–3:6
The Son of Man is master even of the Sabbath.

One sabbath day Jesus happened to be taking a walk through the cornfields, and his disciples began to pick ears of corn as they went along. And the Pharisees said to him, "Look, why are they doing something on the sabbath day that is forbidden?" And he replied, "Did you ever read what David did in his time of need when he and his followers were hungry—how he went into the house of God when Abiathar was high priest, and ate the loaves of offering which only the priests are allowed to eat, and how he also gave some to the men with him?"

And he said to them, "The sabbath was made for man, not man for the sabbath; so the Son of Man is master even of the sabbath."

He went again into a synagogue, and there was a man there who had a withered hand. And they were watching him to see if he could cure him on the sabbath day, hoping for something to use against him. He said to the man with the withered hand, "Stand up out in the middle!" Then he said to them, "Is it against the law on the sabbath day to do good, or to do evil; to save life, or to kill?" But they said nothing. Then, grieved to find them so obstinate, he looked angrily round at them, and said to the man, "Stretch out your hand." He stretched it out and his hand was better. The Pharisees went out and at once began to plot with the Herodians against him, discussing how to destroy him.

This is the Gospel of the Lord.

10th Sunday of the Year

First Reading Gen 3:9–15

I will make you enemies of each other: you and the woman, your offspring and her offspring.

The Lord God called to the man. "Where are you?" he asked, "I heard the sound of you in the garden;" he replied "I was afraid because I was naked, so I hid." "Who told you that you were naked?" he asked "Have you been eating of the tree I forbade you to eat?" The man replied, "It was the woman you put with me; she gave me the fruit, and I ate it." Then the Lord God asked the woman, "What is this you have done?" The woman replied, "The serpent tempted me and I ate."

Then the Lord God said to the serpent, "Because you have done this,

"Be accursed beyond all cattle,
all wild beasts.
You shall crawl on your belly and eat dust
every day of your life.
I will make you enemies of each other:
you and the woman,
your offspring and her offspring.
It will crush your head
and you will strike its heel."

This is the word of the Lord.

Responsorial Psalm Ps 129. R. v. 7

1. Out of the depths I cry to you, O Lord,
Lord, hear my voice!
O let your ears be attentive
to the voice of my pleading.

Response
With the Lord there is mercy
and fullness of redemption.

2. If you, O Lord, should mark our guilt,
Lord, who would survive?
But with you is found forgiveness:
for this we revere you. (*R.*)

3. My soul is waiting for the Lord,
I count on his word.
My soul is longing for the Lord
more than watchman for daybreak. (*R.*)

4. Because with the Lord there is mercy
and fullness of redemption,
Israel indeed he will redeem
from all its iniquity. (*R.*)

Second Reading   2 Cor 4:13–5:1
We believe and therefore we also speak.

As we have the same spirit of faith that is mentioned in
scripture—I believed, and therefore I spoke—we too
believe and therefore we too speak, knowing that he who
raised the Lord Jesus to life will raise us with Jesus in our
turn, and put us by his side and you with us. You see, all
this is for your benefit, so that the more grace is multiplied
among people, the more thanksgiving there will be, to the
glory of God.

That is why there is no weakening on our part, and
instead, though this outer man of ours may be falling
into decay, the inner man is renewed day by day. Yes,
the troubles which are soon over, though they weigh
little, train us for the carrying of a weight of eternal glory
which is out of all proportion to them. And so we have no

eyes for things that are visible, but only for things that are invisible; for visible things last only for a time, and the invisible things are eternal.

For we know that when the tent that we live in on earth is folded up, there is a house built by God for us, an everlasting home not made by human hands, in the heavens.

This is the word of the Lord.

Alleluia   See pp. 184–6.

Gospel   Mk 3:20–35
It is the end of Satan.

Jesus went home with his disciples, and such a crowd collected that they could not even have a meal. When his relatives heard of this, they set out to take charge of him, convinced he was out of his mind.

The scribes who had come down from Jerusalem were saying, "Beelzebul is in him," and, "It is through the prince of devils that he casts devils out." So he called them to him and spoke to them in parables, "How can Satan cast out Satan? If a kingdom is divided against itself, that kingdom cannot last. And if a household is divided against itself, that household can never stand. Now if Satan has rebelled against himself and is divided, he cannot stand either—it is the end of him. But no one can make his way into a strong man's house and burgle his property unless he has tied up the strong man first. Only then can he burgle his house.

"I tell you solemnly, all men's sins will be forgiven, and all their blasphemies; but let anyone blaspheme against the Holy Spirit and he will never have forgiveness: he is guilty of an eternal sin." This was because they were saying, "An unclean spirit is in him."

His mother and brothers now arrived and, standing outside, sent in a message asking for him. A crowd was sitting round him at the time the message was passed to him, "Your mother and brothers and sisters are outside asking for you." He replied, "Who are my mother and my brothers?" And looking round at those sitting in a circle about him, he said, "Here are my mother and my brothers. Any one who does the will of God, that person is my brother and sister and mother."

This is the Gospel of the Lord.

11th Sunday of the Year

First Reading   Ezek 17:22—24
I make low trees grow.

The Lord says this:
"From the top of the cedar,
from the highest branch I will take a shoot
and plant it myself on a very high mountain.
I will plant it on the high mountain of Israel.
It will sprout branches and bear fruit,
and become a noble cedar.
Every kind of bird will live beneath it,
every winged creature rest in the shade of its branches.
And every tree of the field will learn that I, the Lord, am
    the one
who stunts tall trees and makes the low ones grow,
who withers green trees and makes the withered green.
I, the Lord, have spoken, and I will do it."

This is the word of the Lord.

Responsorial Psalm   Ps 91:2—3.13—16. *R*. v. 2

1. It is good to give thanks to the Lord
to make music to your name, O Most High,

to proclaim your love in the morning
and your truth in the watches of the night.

Response
It is good to give you thanks, O Lord.

2. The just will flourish like the palm-tree
and grow like a Lebanon cedar. (*R.*)

3. Planted in the house of the Lord
they will flourish in the courts of our God,
still bearing fruit when they are old,
still full of sap, still green,
to proclaim that the Lord is just.
In him, my rock, there is no wrong. (*R.*)

Second Reading   2 Cor 5:6–10
Whether we are living in the body or exiled from it, we are intent on pleasing the Lord.

We are always full of confidence, then, when we remember that to live in the body means to be exiled from the Lord, going as we do by faith and not by sight—we are full of confidence, I say, and actually want to be exiled from the body and make our home with the Lord. Whether we are living in the body or exiled from it, we are intent on pleasing him. For all the truth about us will be brought out in the law court of Christ, and each of us will get what he deserves for the things he did in the body, good or bad.
   This is the word of the Lord.

Alleluia   See pp. 184–6.

Gospel   Mk 4:26–34
It is the smallest of all the seeds; yet it grows into the
biggest shrub of them all.

Jesus said, "This is what the kingdom of God is like. A
man throws seed on the land. Night and day, while he
sleeps, when he is awake, the seed is sprouting and
growing; how, he does not know. Of its own accord the
land produces first the shoot, then the ear, then the full
grain in the ear. And when the crop is ready, he loses no
time: he starts to reap because the harvest has come."

He also said, "What can we say the kingdom of God
is like? What parable can we find for it? It is like a mustard
seed which at the time of its sowing in the soil is the
smallest of all the seeds on earth; yet once it is sown it
grows into the biggest shrub of them all and puts out big
branches so that the birds of the air can shelter in its
shade."

Using many parables like these, he spoke the word to
them, so far as they were capable of understanding it. He
would not speak to them except in parables, but he
explained everything to his disciples when they were alone.

This is the Gospel of the Lord.

12th Sunday of the Year

First Reading   Job 38:1.8–11
Here your proud waves shall break.

Then from the heart of the tempest the Lord gave Job his
answer. He said:
Who pent up the sea behind closed doors
when it leapt tumultuous out of the womb,

when I wrapped it in a robe of mist
and made black clouds its swaddling bands;
when I marked the bounds it was not to cross
and made it fast with a bolted gate?
Come thus far, I said, and no farther:
here your proud waves shall break.
    This is the word of the Lord.

Responsorial Psalm   Ps 106:23–26.28–31. *R.* v. 1

1. Some sailed to the sea in ships
to trade on the mighty waters.
These men have seen the Lord's deeds.
the wonders he does in the deep.

   Response
   O give thanks to the Lord,
   for his love endures for ever.

   Alternative Response
   Alleluia !

2. For he spoke; he summoned the gale.
tossing the waves of the sea
up to heaven and back into the deep;
their soul melted away in their distress. (*R.*)

3. Then they cried to the Lord in their need
and he rescued them from their distress.
He stilled the storm to a whisper:
all the waves of the sea were hushed. (*R.*)

4. They rejoiced because of the calm
and he led them to the haven they desired.
Let them thank the Lord for his love,
the wonders he does for men. (*R.*)

Second Reading   2 Cor 5 :14–17
Now the new creation is here.

The love of Christ overwhelms us when we reflect that
if one man has died for all, then all men should be dead ;
and the reason he died for all was so that living men should
live no longer for themselves, but for him who died and
was raised to life for them.

From now onwards, therefore, we do not judge anyone
by the standards of the flesh. Even if we did once know
Christ in the flesh, that is not how we know him now. And
for anyone who is in Christ, there is a new creation ; the
old creation has gone, and now the new one is here.

This is the word of the Lord.

Alleluia   See pp. 184–6.

Gospel   Mk 4 :35–41
Who can this be ? Even the wind and the sea obey him.

With the coming of evening, Jesus said to his disciples,
"Let us cross over to the other side." And leaving the
crowd behind they took him, just as he was, in the boat ;
and there were other boats with him. Then it began to
blow a gale and the waves were breaking into the boat so
that it was almost swamped. But he was in the stern, his
head on the cushion, asleep. They woke him and said to
him, "Master, do you not care ? We are going down !" And
he woke up and rebuked the wind and said to the sea,
"Quiet now ! Be calm !" And the wind dropped, and all was
calm again. Then he said to them, "Why are you so
frightened ? How is it that you have no faith ?" They were
filled with awe and said to one another, "Who can this be ?
Even the wind and the sea obey him."

This is the Gospel of the Lord.

13th Sunday of the Year

First Reading   Wis 1 :13–15 ; 2 :23–24
It was the devil's envy that brought death into the world.

Death was not God's doing,
he takes no pleasure in the extinction of the living.
To be—for this he created all ;
the world's created things have health in them,
in them no fatal poison can be found,
and Hades holds no power on earth :
for virtue is undying.
Yet God did make man imperishable,
he made him in the image of his own nature ;
it was the devil's envy that brought death into the world,
as those who are his partners will discover.
    This is the word of the Lord.

Responsorial Psalm   Ps 29 :2 . 4–6 . 11–13. *R*. v. 2

1. I will praise you, Lord, you have rescued me
and have not let my enemies rejoice over me.
O Lord, you have raised my soul from the dead,
restored me to life from those who sink into the grave.

Response
I will praise you, Lord, you have rescued me.

2. Sing psalms to the Lord, you who love him,
give thanks to his holy name.
His anger lasts but a moment ; his favour through life.
At night there are tears, but joy comes with dawn. (*R.*)

3. The Lord listened and had pity.
The Lord came to my help.
For me you have changed my mourning into dancing,
O Lord my God, I will thank you for ever. (*R.*)

Second Reading   2 Cor 8 : 7 . 9 . 13–15

In giving relief to others, balance what happens to be your surplus now against their present need.

You always have the most of everything—of faith, of eloquence, of understanding, of keenness for any cause, and the biggest share of our affection—so we expect you to put the most into this work of mercy too. Remember how generous the Lord Jesus was: he was rich, but he became poor for your sake, to make you rich out of his poverty. This does not mean that to give relief to others you ought to make things difficult for yourselves: it is a question of balancing what happens to be your surplus now against their present need, and one day they may have something to spare that will supply your own need. That is how we strike a balance: as scripture says: The man who gathered much had none too much, the man who gathered little did not go short.

This is the word of the Lord.

Alleluia   See pp. 184-6.

Gospel   Mk 5 : 21–43

Little girl, I tell you to get up.

When Jesus had crossed in the boat to the other side, a large crowd gathered round him and he stayed by the lakeside. Then one of the synagogue officials came up, Jairus by name, and seeing him, fell at his feet and pleaded with him earnestly, saying, "My little daughter is desperately sick. Do come and lay your hands on her to make her better and save her life." Jesus went with him and a large crowd followed him; they were pressing all round him.

Now there was a woman who had suffered from a haemorrhage for twelve years; after long and painful treatment under various doctors, she had spent all she had without being any the better for it, in fact, she was getting worse. She had heard about Jesus, and she came up behind him through the crowd and touched his cloak. "If I can touch even his clothes," she had told herself "I shall be well again." And the source of the bleeding dried up instantly, and she felt in herself that she was cured of her complaint. Immediately aware that power had gone out from him, Jesus turned round in the crowd and said, "Who touched my clothes?" His disciples said to him, "You see how the crowd is pressing round you and yet you say, 'Who touched me?'" But he continued to look all round to see who had done it. Then the woman came forward, frightened and trembling because she knew what had happened to her, and she fell at his feet and told him the whole truth. "My daughter," he said "your faith has restored you to health; go in peace and be free from your complaint."

While he was still speaking some people arrived from the house of the synagogue official to say, "Your daughter is dead: why put the Master to any further trouble?" But Jesus had overheard this remark of theirs and he said to the official, "Do not be afraid; only have faith." And he allowed no one to go with him except Peter and James and John the brother of James. So they came to the official's house and Jesus noticed all the commotion, with people weeping and wailing unrestrainedly. He went in and said to them, "Why all this commotion and crying? The child is not dead, but asleep." But they laughed at him. So he turned them all out and, taking with him the child's father and mother and his own companions, he went into the place where the child lay. And taking the child by the hand he said to her, "Talitha, kum!" which means, "Little girl, I tell you to get up." The little girl got up at once and began to walk about, for she was twelve years old. At this they were overcome with astonishment, and he ordered them strictly not to let anyone know about it, and told them to give her something to eat.

This is the Gospel of the Lord.

14th Sunday of the Year

First Reading   Ezek 2 :2–5
*The sons are defiant and obstinate and they shall know
that there is a prophet among them.*

The spirit came into me and made me stand up, and I heard the Lord speaking to me. He said, "Son of man, I am sending you to the Israelites, to the rebels who have turned against me. Till now they and their ancestors have been in revolt against me. The sons are defiant and obstinate; I am sending you to them, to say, 'The Lord says this.' Whether they listen or not, this set of rebels shall know there is a prophet among them."

This is the word of the Lord.

Responsorial Psalm   Ps 122. *R.* v. 2

1. To you have I lifted up my eyes,
you who dwell in the heavens:
my eyes, like the eyes of slaves
on the hand of their lords.

   Response
   Our eyes are on the Lord
   till he show us his mercy.

2. Like the eyes of a servant
on the hand of her mistress,
so our eyes are on the Lord our God
till he show us his mercy. (*R.*)

3. Have mercy on us, Lord, have mercy.
We are filled with contempt.
Indeed all too full is our soul
with the scorn of the rich,
with the proud man's disdain. (*R.*)

Second Reading   2 Cor 12:7–10
*I shall be very happy to make my weaknesses my special
boast so that the power of Christ may stay over me.*

In view of the extraordinary nature of these revelations,
to stop me from getting too proud I was given a thorn in
the flesh, an angel of Satan to beat me and stop me from
getting too proud! About this thing, I have pleaded with
the Lord three times for it to leave me, but he has said,
"My grace is enough for you: my power is at its best in
weakness." So I shall be very happy to make my weaknesses my special boast so that the power of Christ may
stay over me, and that is why I am quite content with my
weaknesses, and with insults, hardships, persecutions,
and the agonies I go through for Christ's sake. For it is
when I am weak that I am strong.

This is the word of the Lord.

Alleluia   See pp. 184–6.

Gospel   Mk 6:1–6
A prophet is only despised in his own country.

Jesus went to his home town and his disciples accompanied him. With the coming of the sabbath he began

teaching in the synagogue and most of them were astonished when they heard him. They said, "Where did the man get all this? What is this wisdom that has been granted him, and these miracles that are worked through him? This is the carpenter, surely, the son of Mary, the brother of James and Joset and Jude and Simon? His sisters, too, are they not here with us?" And they would not accept him. And Jesus said to them, "A prophet is only despised in his own country, among his own relations and in his own house"; and he could work no miracle there, though he cured a few sick people by laying his hands on them. He was amazed at their lack of faith.

This is the Gospel of the Lord.

15th Sunday of the Year

First Reading   Amos 7 :12–15
Go, prophesy to my people.

To Amos, Amaziah said, "Go away, seer; get back to the land of Judah; earn your bread there, do your pro- phesying there. We want no more prophesying in Bethel; this is the royal sanctuary, the national temple." "I was no prophet, neither did I belong to any of the brotherhoods of prophets," Amos replied to Amaziah, "I was a shepherd, and looked after sycamores: but it was the Lord who took me from herding the flock, and the Lord who said, 'Go, prophesy to my people Israel.' "

This is the word of the Lord.

Responsorial Psalm   Ps 84 :9–14. *R.* v. 8

1. I will hear what the Lord God has to say,
a voice that speaks of peace,

peace for his people.
His help is near for those who fear him
and his glory will dwell in our land.

Response
Let us see, O Lord, your mercy
and give us your saving help.

2. Mercy and faithfulness have met;
justice and peace have embraced.
Faithfulness shall spring from the earth
and justice look down from heaven. (R.)

3. The Lord will make us prosper
and our earth shall yield its fruit.
Justice shall march before him.
and peace shall follow his steps. (R.)

Second Reading   Eph 1 :3–14
Before the world was made, God chose us.

Blessed be God the Father of our Lord Jesus Christ,
who has blessed us with all the spiritual blessings of
    heaven in Christ.
Before the world was made, he chose us, chose us in
    Christ,
to be holy and spotless, and to live through love in his
    presence,
determining that we should become his adopted sons,
    through Jesus Christ
for his own kind purposes,
to make us praise the glory of his grace,
his free gift to us in the Beloved
in whom, through his blood, we gain our freedom, the
    forgiveness of our sins.
Such is the richness of the grace

which he has showered on us
in all wisdom and insight.
He has let us know the mystery of his purpose,
the hidden plan he so kindly made in Christ from the
    beginning
to act upon when the times had run their course to the end:
that he would bring everything together under Christ, as
    head,
everything in the heavens and everything on earth.
And it is in him that we were claimed as God's own,
chosen from the beginning,
under the predetermined plan of the one who guides all
    things
as he decides by his own will;
chosen to be,
for his greater glory,
the people who would put their hopes in Christ before he
    came.
Now you too, in him,
have heard the message of the truth and the good news
    of your salvation,
and have believed it:
and you too have been stamped with the seal of the Holy
    Spirit of the Promise,
the pledge of our inheritance
which brings freedom for those whom God has taken for
    his own,
to make his glory praised.
    This is the word of the Lord.

Alleluia   See pp. 184–6.

Gospel   Mk 6:7–13
He began to send them out.

Jesus summoned the Twelve and began to send them
out in pairs giving them authority over the unclean spirits.

And he instructed them to take nothing for the journey except a staff—no bread, no haversack, no coppers for their purses. They were to wear sandals but, he added, "Do not take a spare tunic." And he said to them, "If you enter a house anywhere, stay there until you leave the district. And if any place does not welcome you and people refuse to listen to you, as you walk away shake off the dust from under your feet as a sign to them." So they set off to preach repentance ; and they cast out many devils, and anointed many sick people with oil and cured them.

This is the Gospel of the Lord.

16th Sunday of the Year

First Reading   Jer. 23:1–6
The remnant of my flock I will gather and I will raise up shepherds to look after them.

"Doom for the shepherds who allow the flock of my pasture to be destroyed and scattered—it is the Lord who speaks ! This, therefore, is what the Lord, the God of Israel, says about the shepherds in charge of my people : You have let my flock be scattered and go wandering and have not taken care of them. Right, I will take care of you for your misdeeds—it is the Lord who speaks ! But the remnant of my flock I myself will gather from all the countries where I have dispersed them, and will bring them back to their pastures : they shall be fruitful and increase in numbers. I will raise up shepherds to look after them and pasture them ; no fear, no terror for them any more ; not one shall be lost—it is the Lord who speaks !
"See the days are coming—it is the Lord who speaks—
when I will raise a virtuous Branch for David,
who will reign as true king and be wise,

practising honesty and integrity in the land.
In his days Judah will be saved
and Israel dwell in confidence.
And this is the name he will be called:
The Lord-our-integrity."
    This is the word of the Lord.

Responsorial Psalm   Ps 22. *R*. v. 1

1. The Lord is my shepherd;
there is nothing I shall want.
Fresh and green are the pastures
where he gives me repose.
Near restful waters he leads me,
to revive my drooping spirit.

> *Response*
> The Lord is my shepherd;
> there is nothing I shall want.

2. He guides me along the right path;
he is true to his name.
If I should walk in the valley of darkness
no evil would I fear.
You are there with your crook and your staff;
with these you give me comfort. (*R*.)

3. You have prepared a banquet for me
in the sight of my foes.
My head you have anointed with oil;
my cup is overflowing. (*R*.)

4. Surely goodness and kindness shall follow me
all the days of my life.
In the Lord's own house shall I dwell
for ever and ever.   (*R*.)

Second Reading   Eph 2 :13—18
*Christ Jesus is the peace between us, and has made the
two into one.*

In Christ Jesus, you that used to be so far apart from us
have been brought very close, by the blood of Christ. For
he is the peace between us, and has made the two into
one and broken down the barrier which used to keep
them apart, actually destroying in his own person the
hostility caused by the rules and decrees of the Law. This
was to create one single New Man in himself out of the
two of them and by restoring peace through the cross, to
unite them both in a single Body and reconcile them with
God. In his own person he killed the hostility. Later he
came to bring the good news of peace, peace to you who
were far away and peace to those who were near at hand.
Through him, both of us have in the one Spirit our way to
come to the Father.

This is the word of the Lord.

Alleluia   See pp. 184—6.

Gospel   Mk 6 :30—34
They were like sheep without a shepherd.

The apostles rejoined Jesus and told him all they had done
and taught. Then he said to them, "You must come away
to some lonely place all by yourselves and rest for a while";
for there were so many coming and going that the apostles
had no time even to eat. So they went off in a boat to a
lonely place where they could be by themselves. But
people saw them going, and many could guess where;
and from every town they all hurried to the place on foot
and reached it before them. So as he stepped ashore he
saw a large crowd; and he took pity on them because they

were like sheep without a shepherd, and he set himself to teach them at some length.

This is the Gospel of the Lord.

17th Sunday of the Year

First Reading   2 Kgs 4 :42—44

They will eat and have some left over.

A man came from Baal-shalishah, bringing Elisha, the man of God, bread from the first-fruits, twenty barley loaves and fresh grain in the ear. "Give it to the people to eat," Elisha said. But his servant replied, "How can I serve this to a hundred men?" "Give it to the people to eat" he insisted "for the Lord says this, 'They will eat and have some left over.' " He served them; they ate and had some over, as the Lord had said.

This is the word of the Lord.

Responsorial Psalm   Ps 144 :10—11 . 15—18. *R*. v. 16

1. All your creatures shall thank you, O Lord,
and your friends shall repeat their blessing.
They shall speak of the glory of your reign
and declare your might, O God.

Response
You open wide your hand, O Lord,
and grant our desires.

2. The eyes of all creatures look to you
and you give them their food in due time.
You open wide your hand,
grant the desires of all who live. (*R*.)

3. The Lord is just in all his ways
and loving in all his deeds.
He is close to all who call him,
who call on him from their hearts. (R.)

Second Reading   Eph 4:1–6
One Body, one Lord, one faith, one baptism.

I, the prisoner in the Lord, implore you to lead a life worthy
of your vocation. Bear with one another charitably, in
complete selflessness, gentleness and patience. Do all you
can to preserve the unity of the Spirit by the peace that
binds you together. There is one Body, one Spirit, just as
you were all called into one and the same hope when you
were called. There is one Lord, one faith, one baptism, and
one God who is Father of all, through all and within all.
    This is the word of the Lord.

Alleluia   See pp. 184–6.

Gospel   Jn 6:1–15
*Jesus gave out as much as was wanted to all who were
sitting ready.*

Jesus went off to the other side of the Sea of Galilee—
or of Tiberias—and a large crowd followed him, impressed
by the signs he gave by curing the sick. Jesus climbed
the hillside, and sat down there with his disciples. It was
shortly before the Jewish feast of Passover.
    Looking up, Jesus saw the crowds approaching and
said to Philip, "Where can we buy some bread for these
people to eat?" He only said this to test Philip; he himself
knew exactly what he was going to do. Philip answered,
"Two hundred denarii would only buy enough to give
them a small piece each." One of his disciples, Andrew,

137

Simon Peter's brother, said, "There is a small boy here with five barley loaves and two fish; but what is that between so many?" Jesus said to them, "Make the people sit down." There was plenty of grass there, and as many as five thousand men sat down. Then Jesus took the loaves, gave thanks, and gave them out to all who were sitting ready; he then did the same with the fish, giving out as much as was wanted. When they had eaten enough he said to the disciples, "Pick up the pieces left over, so that nothing gets wasted." So they picked them up, and filled twelve hampers with scraps left over from the meal of five barley loaves. This people, seeing this sign that he had given, said, "This really is the prophet who is to come into the world." Jesus, who could see they were about to come and take him by force and make him king, escaped back to the hills by himself.

This is the Gospel of the Lord.

18th Sunday of the Year

First Reading   Ex 16:2—4.12—15
I will rain down bread for you from the heavens.

The whole community of the sons of Israel began to complain against Moses and Aaron in the wilderness and said to them, "Why did we not die at the Lord's hand in the land of Egypt, when we were able to sit down to pans of meat and could eat bread to our heart's content! As it is, you have brought us to this wilderness to starve this whole company to death!"

Then the Lord said to Moses, "Now I will rain down bread for you from the heavens. Each day the people are to go out and gather the day's portion; I propose to test them in this way to see whether they will follow my law or not."

"I have heard the complaints of the sons of Israel. Say this to them, 'Between the two evenings you shall eat meat, and in the morning you shall have bread to your heart's content. Then you will learn that I, the Lord, am your God.' " And so it came about: quails flew up in the evening, and they covered the camp; in the morning there was a coating of dew all round the camp. When the coating of dew lifted, there on the surface of the desert was a thing delicate, powdery, as fine as hoarfrost on the ground. When they saw this, the sons of Israel said to one another, "What is that?" not knowing what it was. "That" said Moses to them "is the bread the Lord gives you to eat."

This is the word of the Lord.

Responsorial Psalm   Ps 77:3–4.23–25.54. *R.* v. 24

1. The things we have heard and understood,
the things our fathers have told us,
we will tell to the next generation:
the glories of the Lord and his might.

Response
The Lord gave them bread from heaven.

2. He commanded the clouds above
and opened the gates of heaven.
He rained down manna for their food,
and gave them bread from heaven. (*R.*)

3. Mere men ate the bread of angels.
He sent them abundance of food.
He brought them to his holy land,
to the mountain which his right hand had won. (*R.*)

Second Reading   Eph 4:17. 20–24
Put on the new self that has been created in God's way.

I want to urge you in the name of the Lord, not to go on living the aimless kind of life that pagans live. Now that is hardly the way you have learnt from Christ, unless you failed to hear him properly when you were taught what the truth is in Jesus. You must give up your old way of life; you must put aside your old self, which gets corrupted by following illusory desires. Your mind must be renewed by a spiritual revolution so that you can put on the new self that has been created in God's way, in the goodness and holiness of the truth.

This is the word of the Lord.

Alleluia.   See pp. 184–6.

Gospel   Jn 6:24–35
He who comes to me will never be hungry; he who believes in me will never thirst.

When the people saw that neither Jesus nor his disciples were there, they got into boats and crossed to Capernaum to look for Jesus. When they found him on the other side, they said to him, "Rabbi, when did you come here?" Jesus answered:
"I tell you most solemnly,
you are not looking for me
because you have seen the signs
but because you had all the bread you wanted to eat.
Do not work for food that cannot last,
but work for food that endures to eternal life,
the kind of food the Son of Man is offering you,
for on him the Father, God himself, has set his seal."
Then they said to him, "What must we do if we are to

do the works that God wants?" Jesus gave them this answer, "This is working for God: you must believe in the one he has sent." So they said, "What sign will you give to show us that we should believe in you? What work will you do? Our fathers had manna to eat in the desert; as scripture says: He gave them bread from heaven to eat."

Jesus answered:

"I tell you most solemnly,
it was not Moses who gave you bread from heaven,
it is my Father who gives you the bread from heaven,
the true bread;
for the bread of God
is that which comes down from heaven
and gives life to the world."

"Sir," they said "give us that bread always."

Jesus answered:

"I am the bread of life.
He who comes to me will never be hungry;
he who believes in me will never thirst."

This is the Gospel of the Lord.

19th Sunday of the Year

First Reading   1 Kgs 19 : 4—8
Strengthened by the food he walked until he reached the mountain of God.

Elijah went into the wilderness, a day's journey, and sitting under a furze bush wished he were dead. "Lord," he said "I have had enough. Take my life; I am no better than my ancestors." Then he lay down and went to sleep. But an angel touched him and said, "Get up and eat." He looked round, and there at his head was a scone baked on hot stones, and a jar of water. He ate and drank and then lay down again. But the angel of the Lord came back a

141

second time and touched him and said, "Get up and eat, or the journey will be too long for you." So he got up and ate and drank, and strengthened by that food he walked for forty days and forty nights until he reached Horeb, the mountain of God.

This is the word of the Lord.

Responsorial Psalm

Ps 33 :2–9. *R.* v. 9

1. I will bless the Lord at all times,
his praise always on my lips;
in the Lord my soul shall make its boast.
The humble shall hear and be glad.

Response
Taste and see that the Lord is good.

2. Glorify the Lord with me.
Together let us praise his name.
I sought the Lord and he answered me;
from all my terrors he set me free. (*R.*)

3. Look towards him and be radiant;
let your faces not be abashed.
This poor man called; the Lord heard him
and rescued him from all his distress. (*R.*)

4. The angel of the Lord is encamped
around those who revere him, to rescue them.
Taste and see that the Lord is good.
He is happy who seeks refuge in him. (*R.*)

Second Reading

Eph 4 :30–5 :2

Follow Christ by loving as he loved you.

Do not grieve the Holy Spirit of God who has marked you with his seal for you to be set free when the day comes. Never have grudges against others, or lose your temper, or raise your voice to anybody, or call each other names, or allow any sort of spitefulness. Be friends with one another, and kind, forgiving each other as readily as God forgave you in Christ.

Try then, to imitate God, as children of his that he loves, and follow Christ by loving as he loved you, giving himself up in our place as a fragrant offering and a sacrifice to God.

This is the word of the Lord.

Alleluia See pp. 184—6.

Gospel Jn 6:41—51
I am the living bread which has come down from heaven.

The Jews were complaining to each other about Jesus, because he had said, 'I am the bread that came down from heaven." "Surely this is Jesus son of Joseph" they said. "We know his father and mother. How can he now say, 'I have come down from heaven'?" Jesus said in reply, "Stop complaining to each other.
No one can come to me
unless he is drawn by the Father who sent me,
and I will raise him up at the last day.
It is written in the prophets:
They will all be taught by God,
and to hear the teaching of the Father,
and learn from it,
is to come to me.
Not that anybody has seen the Father,
except the one who comes from God:
he has seen the Father.
I tell you most solemnly,
everybody who believes has eternal life.
I am the bread of life.

Your fathers ate the manna in the desert
and they are dead;
but this is the bread that comes down from heaven,
so that a man may eat it and not die.
I am the living bread which has come down from heaven.
Anyone who eats this bread will live for ever;
and the bread that I shall give
is my flesh, for the life of the world."
　This is the Gospel of the Lord.

20th Sunday of the Year

First Reading　　　　　　　　　　　　　Prov 9:1–6
Eat my bread, drink the wine I have prepared for you.

Wisdom has built herself a house,
she has erected her seven pillars,
she has slaughtered her beasts, prepared her wine,
she has laid her table.
She has despatched her maidservants
and proclaimed from the city's heights:
"Who is ignorant? Let him step this way."
To the fool she says,
"Come and eat my bread,
drink the wine I have prepared!
Leave your folly and you will live,
walk in the ways of perception."
　This is the word of the Lord.

Responsorial Psalm　　　　Ps 33:2–3.10–15. *R.* v. 9

1. I will bless the Lord at all times,
his praise always on my lips;

in the Lord my soul shall make its boast.
The humble shall hear and be glad.

Response
Taste and see that the Lord is good.

2. Revere the Lord, you his saints.
They lack nothing, those who revere him.
Strong lions suffer want and go hungry
but those who seek the Lord lack no blessing. (*R.*)

3. Come, children, and hear me
that I may teach you the fear of the Lord.
Who is he who longs for life
and many days, to enjoy his prosperity? (*R.*)

4. Then keep your tongue from evil
and your lips from speaking deceit.
Turn aside from evil and do good;
seek and strive after peace. (*R.*)

Second Reading   Eph 5:15–20
Recognise what is the will of God.

Be very careful about the sort of lives you lead, like
intelligent and not like senseless people. This may be a
wicked age, but your lives should redeem it. And do not
be thoughtless but recognise what is the will of the Lord.
Do not drug yourselves with wine, this is simply dissipa-
tion; be filled with the Spirit. Sing the words and tunes of
the psalms and hymns when you are together, and go on
singing and chanting to the Lord in your hearts, so that
always and everywhere you are giving thanks to God who
is our Father in the name of our Lord Jesus Christ.
    This is the word of the Lord.

Alleluia   See pp. 184–6.

Gospel   Jn 6 :51—58
My flesh is real food and my blood is real drink.

Jesus said to the crowd :
"I am the living bread which has come down from heaven.
Anyone who eats this bread will live for ever ;
and the bread that I shall give
is my flesh, for the life of the world."
   Then the Jews started arguing with one another :
"How can this man give us his flesh to eat ?" they said.
   Jesus replied :
"I tell you most solemnly,
if you do not eat the flesh of the Son of Man
and drink his blood,
you will not have life in you.
Anyone who does eat my flesh and drink my blood
has eternal life,
and I shall raise him up on the last day.
For my flesh is real food
and my blood is real drink.
He who eats my flesh and drinks my blood
lives in me and I live in him.
As I, who am sent by the living Father,
myself draw life from the Father,
so whoever eats me will draw life from me.
This is the bread come down from heaven ;
not like the bread our ancestors ate :
they are dead,
but anyone who eats this bread will live for ever."
   This is the Gospel of the Lord.

21st Sunday of the Year

First Reading   Jos 24:1–2.15–18
We will serve the Lord, for he is our God.

Joshua gathered all the tribes of Israel together at
Shechem; then he called the elders, leaders, judges and
scribes of Israel, and they presented themselves before
God. Then Joshua said to all the people: "If you will not
serve the Lord, choose today whom you wish to serve,
whether the gods that your ancestors served beyond the
River, or the gods of the Amorites in whose land you are
now living. As for me and my House, we will serve the
Lord."
    The people answered, "We have no intention of deserting
the Lord and serving other gods! Was it not the Lord our
God who brought us and our ancestors out of the land of
Egypt, the house of slavery, who worked those great
wonders before our eyes and preserved us all along the
way we travelled and among all the peoples through whom
we journeyed? We too will serve the Lord, for he is our
God."
    This is the word of the Lord.

Responsorial Psalm   Ps 33:2–3.16–23. *R.* v. 9

1. I will bless the Lord at all times,
his praise always on my lips;
in the Lord my soul shall make its boast.
The humble shall hear and be glad.

    Response
    Taste and see that the Lord is good.

2. The Lord turns his face against the wicked
to destroy their remembrance from the earth.
The Lord turns his eyes to the just
and his ears to their appeal. (*R.*)

3. They call and the Lord hears
and rescues them in all their distress.
The Lord is close to the broken-hearted;
those whose spirit is crushed he will save. (*R.*)

4. Many are the trials of the just man
but from them all the Lord will rescue him.
He will keep guard over all his bones,
not one of his bones shall be broken. (*R.*)

5. Evil brings death to the wicked;
those who hate the good are doomed.
The Lord ransoms the souls of his servants.
Those who hide in him shall not be condemned. (*R.*)

Second Reading   Eph 5 :21–32
*This mystery has many implications for Christ and his
Church.*

Give way to one another in obedience to Christ. Wives
should regard their husbands as they regard the Lord,
since as Christ is head of the Church and saves the whole
body, so is a husband the head of his wife; and as the
Church submits to Christ, so should wives to their husbands, in everything. Husbands should love their wives
just as Christ loved the Church and sacrificed himself for
her to make her holy. He made her clean by washing her
in water with a form of words, so that when he took her to
himself she would be glorious, with no speck or wrinkle or
anything like that, but holy and faultless. In the same way,
husbands must love their wives as they love their own
148

bodies ; for a man to love his wife is for him to love himself. A man never hates his own body, but he feeds it and looks after it ; and that is the way Christ treats the Church, because it is his body—and we are its living parts. For this reason, a man must leave his father and mother and be joined to his wife, and the two will become one body. This mystery has many implications ; but I am saying it applies to Christ and the Church.

This is the word of the Lord.

Alleluia See pp. 184–6, especially no. 5.

Gospel Jn 6 :60–69
Who shall we go to ? You have the message of eternal life.

After hearing his doctrine many of the followers of Jesus said, "This is intolerable language. How could anyone accept it ?" Jesus was aware that his followers were complaining about it and said, "Does this upset you ? What if you should see the Son of Man ascend to where he was before ?
"It is the spirit that gives life,
the flesh has nothing to offer.
The words I have spoken to you are spirit
and they are life.
"But there are some of you who do not believe." For Jesus knew from the outset those who did not believe, and who it was that would betray him. He went on, "This is why I told you that no one could come to me unless the Father allows him." After this, many of his disciples left him and stopped going with him.

Then Jesus said to the Twelve, "What about you, do you want to go away too ?" Simon Peter answered, "Lord, who shall we go to ? You have the message of eternal life, and we believe ; we know that you are the Holy One of God."

This is the Gospel of the Lord.

22nd Sunday of the Year

First Reading Deut 4:1—2.6—8

Add nothing to what I command you, keep the commandments of the Lord.

Moses said to the people: "Now, Israel, take notice of the laws and customs that I teach you today, and observe them, that you may have life and may enter and take possession of the land that the Lord the God of your fathers is giving you. You must add nothing to what I command you, and take nothing from it, but keep the commandments of the Lord your God just as I lay them down for you. Keep them, observe them, and they will demonstrate to the peoples your wisdom and understanding. When they come to know of all these laws they will exclaim, 'No other people is as wise and prudent as this great nation.' And indeed, what great nation is there that has its gods so near as the Lord our God is to us whenever we call to him? And what great nation is there that has laws and customs to match this whole Law that I put before you today?"

This is the word of the Lord.

Responsorial Psalm Ps 14:2—5. *R.* v. 1

1. Lord, who shall dwell on your holy mountain?
He who walks without fault;
he who acts with justice
and speaks the truth from his heart.

Response
Lord, who shall be admitted to your tent?

2. He who does no wrong to his brother,
who casts no slur on his neighbour,

who holds the godless in disdain,
but honours those who fear the Lord. (*R.*)

3. He who keeps his pledge, come what may;
who takes no interest on a loan
and accepts no bribes against the innocent.
Such a man will stand firm for ever. (*R.*)

Second Reading　　　　　　　Jas 1 :17–18 . 21–22 . 27
You must do what the word tells you.

It is all that is good, everything that is perfect, which
is given us from above; it comes down from the Father of
all light; with him there is no such thing as alteration, no
shadow of a change. By his own choice he made us his
children by the message of the truth so that we should be
a sort of first-fruits of all that he had created.

Accept and submit to the word which has been planted
in you and can save your souls. But you must do what the
word tells you, and not just listen to it and deceive
yourselves.

Pure, unspoilt religion, in the eyes of God our Father is
this: coming to the help of orphans and widows when
they need it, and keeping oneself uncontaminated by the
world.

This is the word of the Lord.

Alleluia　　　　　　　　　　　See pp. 184–6.

Gospel　　　　　　　　　　Mk 7 :1–8 . 14–15 . 21–23
*You put aside the commandment of God to cling to
human traditions.*

The Pharisees and some of the scribes who had come
from Jerusalem gathered round Jesus, and they noticed
that some of his disciples were eating with unclean hands,

that is, without washing them. For the Pharisees, and the Jews in general, follow the tradition of the elders and never eat without washing their arms as far as the elbow; and on returning from the market place they never eat without first sprinkling themselves. There are also many other observances which have been handed down to them concerning the washing of cups and pots and bronze dishes. So these Pharisees and scribes asked him, "Why do your disciples not respect the tradition of the elders but eat their food with unclean hands?" He answered, "It was of you hypocrites that Isaiah so rightly prophesied in this passage of scripture:

This people honours me only with lip-service,
while their hearts are far from me.
The worship they offer me is worthless,
the doctrines they teach are only human regulations.

You put aside the commandment of God to cling to human traditions."

He called the people to him again and said, "Listen to me, all of you, and understand. Nothing that goes into a man from outside can make him unclean; it is the things that come out of a man that make him unclean. For it is from within, from men's hearts, that evil intentions emerge: fornication, theft, murder, adultery, avarice, malice, deceit, indecency, envy, slander, pride, folly. All these evil things come from within and make a man unclean."

This is the Gospel of the Lord.

23rd Sunday of the Year

First Reading   Isaiah 35 : 4—7
*The ears of the deaf shall be unsealed and the tongues of
the dumb shall be loosed.*

Say to all faint hearts,
"Courage! Do not be afraid.
Look, your God is coming,
vengeance is coming,
the retribution of God;
he is coming to save you."
Then the eyes of the blind shall be opened,
the ears of the deaf unsealed,
then the lame shall leap like a deer
and the tongues of the dumb sing for joy;
for water gushes in the desert,
streams in the wasteland,
the scorched earth becomes a lake,
the parched land springs of water.
   This is the word of the Lord.

Responsorial Psalm   Ps 145 : 7—10. *R.* v. 1

1. It is the Lord who keeps faith for ever,
who is just to those who are oppressed.
It is he who gives bread to the hungry,
the Lord, who sets prisoners free.

   Response
   My soul, give praise to the Lord.

   Alternative Response
   Alleluia!

2. It is the Lord who gives sight to the blind,
who raises up those who are bowed down,
the Lord who loves the just,
the Lord, who protects the stranger. (*R.*)

3. The Lord upholds the widow and orphan,
but thwarts the path of the wicked.
The Lord will reign for ever,
Zion's God, from age to age. Alleluia! (*R.*)

Second Reading   Jas 2:1–5
God chose the poor to be the heirs to the kingdom.

My brothers, do not try to combine faith in Jesus Christ,
our glorified Lord, with the making of distinctions between
classes of people. Now suppose a man comes into your
synagogue, beautifully dressed and with a gold ring on,
and at the same time a poor man comes in, in shabby
clothes, and you take notice of the well-dressed man, and
say, "Come this way to the best seats"; then you tell the
poor man, "Stand over there" or "You can sit on the floor
by my foot-rest." Can't you see that you have used two
different standards in your mind, and turned yourselves
into judges, and corrupt judges at that?

Listen, my dear brothers: it was those who are poor
according to the world that God chose, to be rich in faith
and to be the heirs to the kingdom which he promised to
those who love him.

This is the word of the Lord.

Alleluia   See pp. 184–6.

Gospel   Mk 7:31–37
He makes the deaf hear and the dumb speak.

Returning from the district of Tyre, Jesus went by way of

Sidon towards the Sea of Galilee, right through the Decapolis region. And they brought him a deaf man who had an impediment in his speech; and they asked him to lay his hand on him. He took him aside in private, away from the crowd, put his fingers into the man's ears and touched his tongue with spittle. Then looking up to heaven he sighed; and he said to him, "Ephphatha", that is, "Be opened." And his ears were opened, and the ligament of his tongue was loosened and he spoke clearly. And Jesus ordered them to tell no one about it, but the more he insisted, the more widely they published it. Their admiration was unbounded. "He has done all things well." they said "he makes the deaf hear and the dumb speak."

This is the Gospel of the Lord.

24th Sunday of the Year

First Reading   Isaiah 50:5—9
I offered my back to those who struck me.

The Lord has opened my ear.
For my part, I made no resistance,
neither did I turn away.
I offered my back to those who struck me,
my cheeks to those who tore at my beard;
I did not cover my face
against insult and spittle.
The Lord comes to my help,
so that I am untouched by the insults.
So, too, I set my face like flint;
I know I shall not be shamed.
My vindicator is here at hand. Does anyone start pro-
    ceedings against me?
Then let us go to court together.

Who thinks he has a case against me?
Let him approach me.
The Lord is coming to my help,
who dare condemn me?
This is the word of the Lord.

Responsial Psalm Ps 114:1–6. 8–9. *R*. v. 9

1. Alleluia!
I love the Lord for he has heard
the cry of my appeal;
for he turned his ear to me
in the day when I called him.

Response
I will walk in the presence of the Lord
in the land of the living.

Alternative Response
Alleluia!

2. They surrounded me, the snares of death,
with the anguish of the tomb;
they caught me, sorrow and distress.
I called on the Lord's name.
O Lord my God, deliver me! (*R.*)

3. How gracious is the Lord, and just;
our God has compassion.
The Lord protects the simple hearts;
I was helpless so he saved me. (*R.*)

4. He has kept my soul from death,
my eyes from tears
and my feet from stumbling.
I will walk in the presence of the Lord
in the land of the living. (*R.*)

Second Reading   Jas 2 :14—18
If good works do not go with faith, it is quite dead.

Take the case, my brothers, of someone who has never
done a single good act but claims that he has faith. Will
that faith save him? If one of the brothers or one of the
sisters is in need of clothes and has not enough food to
live on, and one of you says to them, "I wish you well;
keep yourself warm and eat plenty", without giving them
these bare necessities of life, then what good is that?
Faith is like that: if good works do not go with it, it is
quite dead.

This is the way to talk to people of that kind: "You say
you have faith and I have good deeds; I will prove to you
that I have faith by showing you my good deeds—now
you prove to me that you have faith without any good
deeds to show."

This is the word of the Lord.

Alleluia   See pp. 184—6.

Gospel   Mk 8 :27—35
You are the Christ. The Son of Man is destined to suffer
grievously.

Jesus and his disciples left for the villages round Caesarea
Philippi. On the way he put this question to his disciples,
"Who do people say I am?" And they told him. "John the
Baptist," they said "others Elijah; others again, one of the
prophets." "But you," he asked "who do you say I am?"
Peter spoke up and said to him, "You are the Christ." And
he gave them strict orders not to tell anyone about him.

And he began to teach them that the Son of Man was
destined to suffer grievously, to be rejected by the elders
and the chief priests and the scribes, and to be put to death,

and after three days to rise again ; and he said all this quite openly. Then, taking him aside, Peter started to remonstrate with him. But, turning and seeing his disciples, he rebuked Peter and said to him, "Get behind me, Satan ! Because the way you think is not God's way but man's."

He called the people and his disciples to him and said, "If anyone wants to be a follower of mine, let him renounce himself and take up his cross and follow me. For anyone who wants to save his life will lose it ; but anyone who loses his life for my sake, and for the sake of the gospel, will save it."

This is the Gospel of the Lord.

25th Sunday of the Year

First Reading   Wis 2 :12 . 17–20
Let us condemn him to a shameful death.

The godless say to themselves,
"Let us lie in wait for the virtuous man, since he annoys us
and opposes our way of life,
reproaches us for our breaches of the law
and accuses us of playing false to our upbringing.
Let us see if what he says is true,
let us observe what kind of end he himself will have.
If the virtuous man is God's son, God will take his part
and rescue him from the clutches of his enemies.
Let us test him with cruelty and with torture,
and thus explore this gentleness of his
and put his endurance to the proof.
Let us condemn him to a shameful death
since he will be looked after—we have his word for it."
    This is the word of the Lord.

Responsorial Psalm   Ps 53 :3–6 . 8 . *R.* v. 6

1. O God, save me by your name ;
by your power, uphold my cause.
O God, hear my prayer ;
listen to the words of my mouth.

   Response
   The Lord upholds my life.

2. For proud men have risen against me,
ruthless men seek my life.
They have no regard for God. (*R.*)

3. But I have God for my help.
The Lord upholds my life.
I will sacrifice to you with willing heart
and praise your name for it is good (*R.*)

Second Reading   Jas 3 :16–4 :3
*Peacemakers, when they work for peace, sow the seeds
which will bear fruit in holiness.*

Wherever you find jealousy and ambition, you find
disharmony, and wicked things of every kind being done ;
whereas the wisdom that comes down from above is
essentially something pure ; it also makes for peace, and
is kindly and considerate ; it is full of compassion and
shows itself by doing good ; nor is there any trace of
partiality or hypocrisy in it. Peacemakers, when they work
for peace, sow the seeds which will bear fruit in holiness.
   Where do these wars and battles between yourselves
first start ? Isn't it precisely in the desires fighting inside
your own selves ? You want something and you haven't
got it ; so you are prepared to kill. You have an ambition

159

that you cannot satisfy; so you fight to get your way by force. Why you don't have what you want is because you don't pray for it; when you do pray and don't get it, it is because you have not prayed properly, you have prayed for something to indulge your own desires.

This is the word of the Lord.

Alleluia See pp. 184–6.

Gospel Mk 9 :30–37
The Son of Man will be delivered. If anyone wants to be first, he must make himself servant of all.

After leaving the mountain Jesus and his disciples made their way through Galilee; and he did not want anyone to know, because he was instructing his disciples; he was telling them, "The Son of Man will be delivered into the hands of men; they will put him to death; and three days after he has been put to death he will rise again." But they did not understand what he said and were afraid to ask him.

They came to Capernaum, and when he was in the house he asked them, "What were you arguing about on the road?" They said nothing because they had been arguing which of them was the greatest. So he sat down, called the Twelve to him and said, "If anyone wants to be first, he must make himself last of all and servant of all." He then took a little child, set him in front of them, put his arms round him, and said to them, "Anyone who welcomes one of these little children in my name, welcomes me; and anyone who welcomes me welcomes not me but the one who sent me."

This is the Gospel of the Lord.

26th Sunday of the Year

First Reading   Num 11 :25—29
*Are you jealous on my account ? If only the whole people
of the Lord were prophets !*

The Lord came down in the Cloud. He spoke with Moses,
but took some of the spirit that was on him and put it on
the seventy elders. When the spirit came on them they
prophesied, but not again.

Two men had stayed back in the camp ; one was called
Eldad and the other Medad. The spirit came down on
them ; though they had not gone to the Tent, their names
were enrolled among the rest. These began to prophesy in
the camp. The young man ran to tell this to Moses, "Look,"
he said "Eldad and Medad are prophesying in the camp."
Then said Joshua the son of Nun, who had served Moses
from his youth, "My Lord Moses, stop them !" Moses
answered him, "Are you jealous on my account ? If only
the whole people of the Lord were prophets, and the Lord
gave his Spirit to them all !"

This is the word of the Lord.

Responsorial Psalm   Ps 18 :8.10.12—14. *R*. v. 9

1. The law of the Lord is perfect,
it revives the soul.
The rule of the Lord is to be trusted,
it gives wisdom to the simple.

Response
The precepts of the Lord gladden the heart.

2. The fear of the Lord is holy,
abiding for ever.

The decrees of the Lord are truth
and all of them just. (*R.*)

3. So in them your servant finds instruction;
great reward is in their keeping.
But who can detect all his errors?
From hidden faults acquit me. (*R.*)

4. From presumption restrain your servant
and let it not rule me.
Then shall I be blameless,
clean from grave sin. (*R.*)

Second Reading   Jas 5:1–6
Your wealth is all rotting.

An answer for the rich. Start crying, weep for the miseries
that are coming to you. Your wealth is all rotting, your
clothes are all eaten up by moths. All your gold and your
silver are corroding away, and the same corrosion will be
your own sentence, and eat into your body. It was a
burning fire that you stored up as your treasure for the last
days. Labourers mowed your fields, and you cheated them
—listen to the wages that you kept back, calling out;
realise that the cries of the reapers have reached the ears
of the Lord of hosts. On earth you have had a life of comfort
and luxury; in the time of slaughter you went on eating to
your heart's content. It was you who condemned the
innocent and killed them; they offered you no resistance.
   This is the word of the Lord.

Alleluia   See pp. 184–6.

Gospel   Mk 9:38–43.45.47–48
Anyone who is not against us is for us.
If your hand should cause you to sin, cut it off.

John said to Jesus, "Master, we saw a man who is not

one of us casting out devils in your name; and because he was not one of us we tried to stop him." But Jesus said, "You must not stop him: no one who works a miracle in my name is likely to speak evil of me. Anyone who is not against us is for us.

"If anyone gives you a cup of water to drink just because you belong to Christ, then I tell you solemnly, he will most certainly not lose his reward.

"But anyone who is an obstacle to bring down one of these little ones who have faith, would be better thrown into the sea with a great millstone round his neck. And if your hand should cause you to sin, cut it off; it is better for you to enter into life crippled, than to have two hands and go to hell, into the fire that cannot be put out. And if your foot should cause you to sin, cut it off; it is better for you to enter into life lame, than to have two feet and be thrown into hell. And if your eye should cause you to sin, tear it out; it is better for you to enter into the kingdom of God with one eye, than to have two eyes and be thrown into hell where their worm does not die nor their fire go out."

This is the Gospel of the Lord.

27th Sunday of the Year

First Reading   Gen 2:18–24
They become one body.

The Lord God said, "It is not good that the man should be alone. I will make him a helpmate." So from the soil the Lord God fashioned all the wild beasts and all the birds of heaven. These he brought to the man to see what he would call them; each one was to bear the name the man would give it. The man gave names to all the cattle, all the birds of heaven and all the wild beasts. But no helpmate suitable for man was found for him. So the Lord God made the man fall into a deep sleep. And while he slept, he took one of his ribs and enclosed it in flesh. The Lord God built the rib he had taken from the man into a woman, and brought her to the man. The man exclaimed:

"This at last is bone from my bones,
and flesh from my flesh!
This is to be called woman,
for this was taken from man."

This is why a man leaves his father and mother and joins himself to his wife, and they become one body.

This is the word of the Lord.

Responsorial Psalm   Ps 127. *R*. v. 5

1. O blessed are those who fear the Lord
and walk in his ways!
By the labour of your hands you shall eat.
You will be happy and prosper.

 Response
 May the Lord bless us
 all the days of our life.

2. Your wife will be like a fruitful vine
in the heart of your house;
your children like shoots of the olive,
around your table. (*R.*)

3. Indeed thus shall be blessed
the man who fears the Lord.
May the Lord bless you from Zion
in a happy Jerusalem
all the days of your life!
May you see your children's children.
On Israel, peace! (*R.*)

Second Reading Heb 2 :9–11
The one who sanctifies, and the ones who are sanctified
are of the same stock.

We see in Jesus one who was for a short while made
lower than the angels and is now crowned with glory and
splendour because he submitted to death ; by God's grace
he had to experience death for all mankind.

   As it was his purpose to bring a great many of his sons
into glory, it was appropriate that God, for whom everything exists and through whom everything exists, should
make perfect, through suffering, the leader who would take
them to their salvation. For the one who sanctifies, and the
ones who are sanctified, are of the same stock ; that is why
he openly calls them brothers.

   This is the word of the Lord.

Alleluia. See pp. 184–6.

Gospel Mk 10 :2–16
What God has united, man must not divide.

Some Pharisees approached Jesus and asked, "Is it
against the law for a man to divorce his wife ?" They were
testing him. He answered them, "What did Moses command you ?" "Moses allowed us" they said "to draw up
a writ of dismissal and so to divorce." Then Jesus said to
them, "It was because you were so unteachable that he
wrote this commandment for you. But from the beginning
of creation God made them male and female. This is why a
man must leave father and mother, and the two become
one body. They are no longer two, therefore, but one body.
So then, what God has united, man must not divide."
Back in the house the disciples questioned him again about
this, and he said to them, "The man who divorces his wife

and marries another is guilty of adultery against her. And if a woman divorces her husband and marries another she is guilty of adultery too."

People were bringing little children to him, for him to touch them. The disciples turned them away, but when Jesus saw this he was indignant and said to them, "Let the little children come to me; do not stop them; for it is to such as these that the kingdom of God belongs. I tell you solemnly, anyone who does not welcome the kingdom of God like a little child will never enter it." Then he put his arms round them, laid his hands on them and gave them his blessing.

This is the Gospel of the Lord.

28th Sunday of the Year

First Reading   Wis 7:7–11
Compared with wisdom, I held riches as nothing.

I prayed, and understanding was given me;
I entreated, and the spirit of Wisdom came to me.
I esteemed her more than sceptres and thrones;
compared with her, I held riches as nothing.
I reckoned no priceless stone to be her peer,
for compared with her, all gold is a pinch of sand,
and beside her silver ranks as mud.
I loved her more than health or beauty,
preferred her to the light,
since her radiance never sleeps.
In her company all good things came to me,
at her hands riches not to be numbered.
    This is the word of the Lord.

Responsorial Psalm　　　　　　Ps 89 : 12–17. *R.* v. 14

1. Make us know the shortness of our life
that we may gain wisdom of heart.
Lord, relent! Is your anger for ever?
Show pity to your servants.

　Response
　Fill us with your love that we may rejoice.

2. In the morning, fill us with your love;
we shall exult and rejoice all our days.
Give us joy to balance our affliction
for the years when we knew misfortune. (*R.*)

3. Show forth your work to your servants;
let your glory shine on their children.
Let the favour of the Lord be upon us:
give success to the work of our hands. (*R.*)

Second Reading　　　　　　　　Heb 4 : 12–13
The word of God can judge secret emotions and thoughts.

The word of God is something alive and active: it cuts like
any double-edged sword but more finely: it can slip
through the place where the soul is divided from the spirit,
or joints from the marrow; it can judge the secret emotions and thoughts. No created thing can hide from him;
everything is uncovered and open to the eyes of the one
to whom we must give account of ourselves.
　This is the word of the Lord.

Alleluia　　　　　　　　　　　See pp. 184–6.

Gospel   Mk 10:17–30
Go and sell everything you own and follow me.

Jesus was setting out on a journey when a man ran up,
knelt before him and put this question to him, "Good
master, what must I do to inherit eternal life?" Jesus said
to him, "Why do you call me good? No one is good but
God alone. You know the commandments: You must not
kill; You must not commit adultery; You must not steal;
You must not bring false witness; You must not defraud;
Honour your father and mother." And he said to him,
"Master, I have kept all these from my earliest days."
Jesus looked steadily at him and loved him, and he said,
"There is one thing you lack. Go and sell everything you
own and give the money to the poor, and you will have
treasure in heaven; then come, follow me." But his face
fell at these words and he went away sad, for he was a
man of great wealth.

Jesus looked round and said to his disciples, "How hard
it is for those who have riches to enter the kingdom of
God!" The disciples were astounded by these words, but
Jesus insisted, "My children," he said to them "how hard it
it is to enter the kingdom of God! It is easier for a camel to
pass through the eye of a needle than for a rich man to enter
the kingdom of God." They were more astonished than ever.
"In that case" they said to one another "who can be saved?"
Jesus gazed at them. "For men" he said "it is impossible,
but not for God: because everything is possible for God."

Peter took this up. "What about us?" he asked him.
"We have left everything and followed you." Jesus said,
"I tell you solemnly, there is no one who has left house,
brothers, sisters, father, children or land for my sake and
for the sake of the gospel who will not be repaid a
hundred times over, houses, brothers, sisters, mothers,
children and land—not without persecutions—now in this
present time and, in the world to come, eternal life."

This is the Gospel of the Lord.

29th Sunday of the Year

First Reading   Isaiah 53 :10–11
If he offers his life in atonement, he shall see his heirs, he
shall have a long life.

The Lord has been pleased to crush him with suffering.
If he offers his life in atonement,
he shall see his heirs, he shall have a long life
and through him what the Lord wishes will be done.
His soul's anguish over
he shall see the light and be content.
By his sufferings shall my servant justify many,
taking their faults on himself.
    This is the word of the Lord.

Responsorial Psalm   Ps 32 :4–5 . 18–20 . 22 . *R.* v. 22

1. The word of the Lord is faithful
and all his works to be trusted.
The Lord loves justice and right
and fills the earth with his love.

    Response
    May your love be upon us, O Lord,
    as we place all our hope in you.

2. The Lord looks on those who revere him,
on those who hope in his love,
to rescue their souls from death,
to keep them alive in famine. (*R.*)

3. Our soul is waiting for the Lord.

The Lord is our help and our shield.
May your love be upon us, O Lord,
as we place all our hope in you. (*R.*)

Second Reading   Heb 4:14–16
Let us be confident in approaching the throne of grace.

Since in Jesus, the Son of God, we have the supreme high
priest who has gone through to the highest heaven, we
must never let go of the faith that we have professed. For
it is not as if we had a high priest who was incapable of
feeling our weaknesses with us; but we have one who
has been tempted in every way that we are, though he is
without sin. Let us be confident, then, in approaching the
throne of grace, that we shall have mercy from him and
find grace when we are in need of help.
    This is the word of the Lord.

Alleluia   See pp. 184–6.

Gospel   Mk 10:35–45
The Son of Man came to give his life as a ransom for many.

James and John, the sons of Zebedee, approached Jesus.
"Master," they said to him "we want you to do us a favour."
He said to them, "What is it you want me to do for you?"
They said to him, "Allow us to sit one at your right hand and
the other at your left in your glory." "You do not know
what you are asking" Jesus said to them. "Can you drink
the cup that I must drink, or be baptised with the baptism
with which I must be baptised?" They replied, "We can."
Jesus said to them, "The cup that I must drink you shall
drink, and with the baptism with which I must be baptised
you shall be baptised, but as for seats at my right hand or
my left, these are not mine to grant; they belong to those
to whom they have been allotted."

When the other ten heard this they began to feel indignant with James and John, so Jesus called them to him and said to them, "You know that among the pagans their so-called rulers lord it over them, and their great men make their authority felt. This is not to happen among you. No; anyone who wants to become great among you must be your servant, and anyone who wants to be first among you must be slave to all. For the Son of Man himself did not come to be served but to serve, and to give his life as a ransom for many."

This is the Gospel of the Lord.

30th Sunday of the Year

First Reading   Jer 31 :7–9
I will comfort the blind and the lame as I lead them back.

The Lord says this :
Shout with joy for Jacob !
Hail the chief of nations !
Proclaim ! Praise ! Shout :
"The Lord has saved his people,
the remnant of Israel !"
See, I will bring them back
from the land of the North
and gather them from the far ends of earth :
all of them : the blind and the lame,
women with child, women in labour :
a great company returning here.
They had left in tears,
I will comfort them as I lead them back :
I will guide them to streams of water,
by a smooth path where they will not stumble.
For I am a father to Israel,

and Ephraim is my first-born son.
  This is the word of the Lord.

Responsorial Psalm   Ps 125. *R.* 3

1. When the Lord delivered Zion from bondage,
It seemed like a dream.
Then was our mouth filled with laughter,
on our lips there were songs.

  Response
  What marvels the Lord worked for us!
  Indeed we were glad.

2. The heathens themselves said: "What marvels
the Lord worked for them!"
What marvels the Lord worked for us!
Indeed we were glad. (*R.*)

3. Deliver us, O Lord, from our bondage
as streams in dry land.
Those who are sowing in tears
will sing when they reap. (*R.*)

4. They go out, they go out, full of tears,
carrying seed for the sowing:
they come back, they come back, full of song,
carrying their sheaves. (*R.*)

Second Reading   Heb 5:1–6
You are a priest of the order of Melchizedek, and for ever.

Every high priest has been taken out of mankind and is
appointed to act for men in their relations with God, to
offer gifts and sacrifices for sins; and so he can sympathise
172

with those who are ignorant or uncertain because he too lives in the limitations of weakness. That is why he has to make sin offerings for himself as well as for the people. No one takes this honour on himself, but each one is called by God, as Aaron was. Nor did Christ give himself the glory of becoming high priest, but he had it from the one who said to him: You are my son, today I have become your father: and in another text: You are a priest of the order of Melchizedek, and for ever.

This is the word of the Lord.

Alleluia   See pp. 184–6.

Gospel   Mk 10:46–52
Master, let me see again.

As Jesus left Jericho with his disciples and a large crowd, Bartimaeus (that is, the son of Timaeus), a blind beggar, was sitting at the side of the road. When he heard that it was Jesus of Nazareth, he began to shout and to say, "Son of David, Jesus, have pity on me." And many of them scolded him and told him to keep quiet, but he only shouted all the louder, "Son of David, have pity on me." Jesus stopped and said, "Call him here." So they called the blind man. "Courage," they said "get up; he is calling you." So throwing off his cloak, he jumped up and went to Jesus. Then Jesus spoke, "What do you want me to do for you?" "Rabbuni," the blind man said to him "Master, let me see again." Jesus said to him, "Go; your faith has saved you." And immediately his sight returned and he followed him along the road.

This is the Gospel of the Lord.

31st Sunday of the Year

First Reading   Deut 6:2–6
Listen, Israel: You shall love the Lord your God with all your heart.

Moses said to the people: "If you fear the Lord your God all the days of your life and if you keep all his laws and commandments which I lay on you, you will have a long life, you and your son and your grandson. Listen then, Israel, keep and observe what will make you prosper and give you great increase, as the Lord God of your fathers has promised you, giving you a land where milk and honey flow.

"Listen, Israel: The Lord our God is the one Lord. You shall love the Lord your God with all your heart, with all your soul, with all your strength. Let these words I urge on you today be written on your heart."

This is the word of the Lord.

Responsorial Psalm   Ps 17:2–4.47.51. *R.* v. 2

1. I love you, Lord, my strength,
my rock, my fortress, my saviour.
My God is the rock where I take refuge;
my shield, my mighty help, my stronghold.
The Lord is worthy of all praise:
when I call I am saved from my foes.

    Response
    I love you, Lord, my strength.

2. For life to the Lord, my rock!
Praised be the God who saves me.

He has given great victories to his king
and shown his love for his anointed. (*R.*)

Second Reading   Heb 7 :23–28
*Because he remains for ever, Christ can never lose his
priesthood.*

There used to be a great number of those other priests,
because death put an end to each one of them; but this
one, Christ, because he remains for ever, can never lose
his priesthood. It follows, then, that his power to save is
utterly certain, since he is living for ever to intercede for
all who come to God through him.

To suit us, the ideal high priest would have to be holy,
innocent and uncontaminated, beyond the influence of
sinners, and raised up above the heavens; one who would
not need to offer sacrifices every day, as the other high
priests do for their own sins and then for those of the
people, because he has done this once and for all by
offering himself. The Law appoints high priests who are
men subject to weakness; but the promise on oath, which
came after the Law, appointed the Son who is made
perfect for ever.

This is the word of the Lord.

Alleluia   See pp. 184–6.

Gospel   Mk 12 :28–34
This is the first commandment. The second is like it.

One of the scribes now came up and put a question to
him, "Which is the first of all the commandments?" Jesus
replied, "This is the first: Listen, Israel, the Lord our God
is the one Lord, and you must love the Lord your God with
all your heart, with all your soul, with all your mind and

with all your strength. The second is this : You must love your neighbour as yourself. There is no commandment greater than these." The scribe said to him, "Well spoken, Master ; what you have said is true : that he is one and there is no other. To love him with all your heart, with all your understanding and strength and to love your neighbour as yourself, this is far more important than any holocaust or sacrifice." Jesus, seeing how wisely he had spoken, said, "You are not far from the kingdom of God." And after that no one dared to question him any more.

This is the Gospel of the Lord.

32nd Sunday of the Year

First Reading 1 Kgs 17 :10–16
The widow made a little scone from her meal and brought it to Elijah.

Elijah went off to Sidon. And when he reached the city gate, there was a widow gathering sticks ; addressing her he said, "Please bring a little water in a vessel for me to drink." She was setting off to bring it when he called after her. "Please" he said "bring me a scrap of bread in your hand." "As the Lord your God lives," she replied "I have no baked bread, but only a handful of meal in a jar and a little oil in a jug ; I am just gathering a stick or two to go and prepare this for myself and my son to eat, and then we shall die." But Elijah said to her, "Do not be afraid, go and do as you have said ; but first make a little scone of it for me and bring it to me, and then make some for yourself and for your son. For thus the Lord speaks, the God of Israel :

'Jar of meal shall not be spent,
jug of oil shall not be emptied,

before the day when the Lord sends
rain on the face of the earth.' "

The woman went and did as Elijah told her and they ate
the food, she, himself and her son. The jar of meal was not
spent nor the jug of oil emptied, just as the Lord had foretold through Elijah.

This is the word of the Lord.

Responsorial Psalm   Ps 145 :7–10. *R*. v. 2

1. It is the Lord who keeps faith for ever,
who is just to those who are oppressed.
It is he who gives bread to the hungry,
the Lord, who sets prisoners free.

Response
My soul, give praise to the Lord.

Alternative Response
Alleluia !

2. It is the Lord who gives sight to the blind,
who raises up those who are bowed down.
It is the Lord who loves the just,
the Lord, who protects the stranger. (*R.*)

3. He upholds the widow and orphan
but thwarts the path of the wicked.
The Lord will reign for ever,
Zion's God, from age to age. (*R.*)

Second Reading   Heb 9 :24–28
*Christ offers himself only once to take the faults of many
on himself.*

It is not as though Christ had entered a man-made sanctuary which was only modelled on the real one ; but it was

177

heaven itself, so that he could appear in the actual presence of God on our behalf. And he does not have to offer himself again and again, like the high priest going into the sanctuary year after year with the blood that is not his own, or else he would have had to suffer over and over again since the world began. Instead of that, he has made his appearance once and for all, now at the end of the last age, to do away with sin by sacrificing himself. Since men only die once, and after that comes judgement, so Christ, too, offers himself only once to take the faults of many on himself, and when he appears a second time, it will not be to deal with sin but to reward with salvation those who are waiting for him.

This is the word of the Lord.

Alleluia   See p. 186 nos. 14, 15, 16.

Gospel   Mk 12 :38–44
This poor widow has put in more than all.

In his teaching Jesus said, "Beware of the scribes who like to walk about in long robes, to be greeted obsequiously in the market squares, to take the front seats in the synagogues and the places of honour at banquets; these are the men who swallow the property of widows, while making a show of lengthy prayers. The more severe will be the sentence they receive."

He sat down opposite the treasury and watched the people putting money into the treasury, and many of the rich put in a great deal. A poor widow came and put in two small coins, the equivalent of a penny. Then he called his disciples and said to them, "I tell you solemnly, this poor widow has put more in than all who have contributed to the treasury; for they have all put in money they had over, but she from the little she had has put in everything she possessed, all she had to live on."

This is the Gospel of the Lord.

33rd Sunday of the Year

First Reading   Dan 12 :1–3
When that time comes, your own people will be spared.

"At that time Michael will stand up, the great prince who
mounts guard over your people. There is going to be a
time of great distress, unparalleled since nations first
came into existence. When that time comes, your own
people will be spared, all those whose names are found
written in the Book. Of those who lie sleeping in the dust
of the earth many will awake, some to everlasting life,
some to shame and everlasting disgrace. The learned will
shine as brightly as the vault of heaven, and those who have
instructed many in virtue, as bright as stars for all eternity."
   This is the word of the Lord.

Responsorial Psalm   Ps 15 :5 . 8–11. *R.* v. 1

1. O Lord, it is you who are my portion and cup ;
It is you yourself who are my prize.
I keep the Lord ever in my sight :
since he is at my right hand, I shall stand firm.

   Response
   Preserve me, God, I take refuge in you.

2. And so my heart rejoices, my soul is glad ;
even my body shall rest in safety.
For you will not leave my soul among the dead,
nor let your beloved know decay. (*R.*)

3. You will show me the path of life,
the fullness of joy in your presence,
at your right hand happiness for ever. (*R.*)

Second Reading   Heb 10:11–14.18
By virtue of one single offering, he has achieved the eternal
perfection of all whom he is sanctifying.

All the priests stand at their duties every day, offering over
and over again the same sacrifices which are quite incapable of taking sins away. Christ, on the other hand, has
offered one single sacrifice for sins, and then taken his
place for ever, at the right hand of God, where he is now
waiting until his enemies are made into a footstool for
him. By virtue of that one single offering, he has achieved
the eternal perfection of all whom he is sanctifying. When
all sins have been forgiven, there can be no more sin
offerings.
   This is the word of the Lord.

Alleluia   See p. 186, nos. 14, 15, 16.

Gospel   Mk 13:24–32
He will gather his chosen from the four winds.

Jesus said to his disciples: "In those days, after that
time of distress, the sun will be darkened, the moon will
lose its brightness, the stars will come falling from heaven
and the powers in the heavens will be shaken. And then
they will see the Son of Man coming in the clouds with
great power and glory; then too he will send the angels to
gather his chosen from the four winds, from the ends of
the world to the ends of heaven.
   "Take the fig tree as a parable: as soon as its twigs grow
supple and its leaves come out, you know that summer is
near. So with you when you see these things happening:
know that he is near, at the very gates. I tell you solemnly,
before this generation has passed away all these things

will have taken place. Heaven and earth will pass away, but my words will not pass away.

"But as for that day or hour, nobody knows it, neither the angels of heaven, nor the Son ; no one but the Father."

This is the Gospel of the Lord.

34th or Last Sunday of the Year

Solemnity of Our Lord Jesus Christ
Universal King

First Reading   Dan 7 :13–14
His sovereignty is an eternal sovereignty.

"I gazed into the visions of the night.
And I saw, coming on the clouds of heaven,
one like a son of man.
He came to the one of great age
and was led into his presence.
On him was conferred sovereignty,
glory and kingship,
and men of all peoples, nations and languages became
 his servants.
His sovereignty is an eternal sovereignty
which shall never pass away,
nor will his empire ever be destroyed."

This is the word of the Lord.

Responsorial Psalm   Ps 92 :1–2. 5. *R.* v. 1

1. The Lord is king, with majesty enrobed ;
the Lord has robed himself with might,
he has girded himself with power.

Response
The Lord is king, with majesty enrobed.

2. The word you made firm, not to be moved ;
your throne has stood firm from of old.
From all eternity, O Lord, you are. (*R.*)

3. Truly your decrees are to be trusted.
Holiness is fitting to your house,
O Lord, until the end of time. (*R.*)

Second Reading   Apoc 1 :5–8
Ruler of the kings of the earth . . . he made us a line of kings, priests to serve his God.

Grace and peace to you from Jesus Christ, the faithful witness, the First-born from the dead, the Ruler of the kings of the earth. He loves us and has washed away our sins with his blood, and made us a line of kings, priests to serve his God and Father ; to him, then, be glory and power for ever and ever. Amen. It is he who is coming on the clouds ; everyone will see him, even those who pierced him, and all the races of the earth will mourn over him. This is the truth. Amen. "I am the Alpha and the Omega" says the Lord God, who is, who was, and who is to come, the Almighty.

This is the word of the Lord.

Alleluia   Mk 11 :10

Alleluia, alleluia !
Blessings on him who comes in the name of the Lord !
Blessings on the coming kingdom of our father David !
Alleluia !

Gospel Jn 18:33–37

It is you who say that I am a king.

"Are you the king of the Jews?" Pilate asked. Jesus replied, "Do you ask this of your own accord, or have others spoken to you about me?" Pilate answered, "Am I a Jew? It is your own people and the chief priests who have handed you over to me: what have you done?" Jesus replied, "Mine is not a kingdom of this world; if my kingdom were of this world, my men would have fought to prevent my being surrendered to the Jews. But my kingdom is not of this kind." "So you are a king then?" said Pilate. "It is you who say it" answered Jesus. "Yes, I am a king. I was born for this, I came into the world for this: to bear witness to the truth; and all who are on the side of truth listen to my voice."

This is the Gospel of the Lord.

Alleluia

For use *ad libitum* on the Sundays of the Year.

1. Alleluia, alleluia! (1 Sam 3:9; Jn 6:68)
Speak, Lord, your servant is listening:
you have the message of eternal life.
Alleluia!

2. Alleluia, alleluia! (Mt 11:25)
Blessed are you, Father,
Lord of heaven and earth,
for revealing the mysteries of the kingdom
to mere children.
Alleluia!

3. Alleluia, alleluia! (Lk 19:38)
Blessings on the King who comes,
in the name of the Lord!
Peace in heaven
and glory in the highest heavens!
Alleluia!

4. Alleluia, alleluia! (Jn 1:12.14)
The Word was made flesh and lived among us;
to all who did accept him
he gave power to become children of God.
Alleluia!

5. Alleluia, alleluia! (Jn 6:63.68)
Your words are spirit, Lord,
and they are life:
you have the message of eternal life.
Alleluia!

(Jn 8:12)

6. Alleluia, alleluia!
I am the light of the world, says the Lord,
anyone who follows me
will have the light of life.
Alleluia!

(Jn 10:27)

7. Alleluia, alleluia!
The sheep that belong to me listen to my voice,
says the Lord,
I know them and they follow me.
Alleluia!

(Jn 14:5)

8. Alleluia, alleluia!
I am the Way, the Truth and the Life, says the Lord;
no one can come to the Father except through me.
Alleluia!

(Jn 14:23)

9. Alleluia, alleluia!
If anyone loves me he will keep my word,
and my Father will love him,
and we shall come to him.
Alleluia!

(Jn 15:15)

10. Alleluia, alleluia!
I call you friends, says the Lord,
because I have made known to you
everything I have learnt from my Father.
Alleluia!

(Jn 17:17)

11. Alleluia, alleluia!
Your word is truth, O Lord,
consecrate us in the truth.
Alleluia!

ALLELUIA FOR SUNDAYS OF YEAR

(Acts 16:14)

12. Alleluia, alleluia!
Open our heart, O Lord,
to accept the words of your Son.
Alleluia!

(Eph 1:17.18)

13. Alleluia, alleluia!
May the Father of our Lord Jesus Christ
enlighten the eyes of our mind.
so that we can see what hope his call holds for us.
Alleluia!

For the last Sundays of the Year.

(Mt 24:22.44)

14. Alleluia, alleluia!
Stay awake and stand ready,
because you do not know the hour
when the Son of Man is coming.
Alleluia!

(Lk 21:36)

15. Alleluia, alleluia!
Stay awake, praying at all times
for the strength to stand with confidence
before the Son of Man.
Alleluia!

(Apoc. 2:10)

16 Alleluia, alleluia!
Even if you have to die, says the Lord,
keep faithful, and I will give you
the crown of life.
Alleluia!